The
SOUL CAFÉ

David McLean

THE SOUL CAFÉ

Copyright © 2001, David Malcolm Ian McLean

Published by The Wyndham Press
Unit 64, 2665 Thomas Street,
Mississauga, ON L5M 6G6
905 567-5009

Special Discounts on bulk quantities of this title are available
to universities, corporations, professional associations,
and other organizations. For further information, please contact the
publisher at Unit 64, 2665 Thomas Street, Mississauga, ON L5M
6G6 Phone 905 567-5009; Fax: 905 567-5305.

First Edition First Printing 2001

National Library of Canada Cataloguing in Publication Data

McLean, David Malcolm Ian, 1963-
The soul café: seeking wholeness in life one cup at a time

ISBN 0-9688700-0-7

1. Title.

PS8575.L38925S69 2001
   C813'.6 C2001-901098-2
PR9199.4.M34S69 2001

This book is dedicated to each of those whose souls have fallen victim to the false promises of life.

May you soon find your way to peace and happiness.

Table of Contents

Acknowledgements

In the same way that a book is a collection of words bound together with thought and emotion, a life is a collection of experiences wrapped with love, faith and relationships. This book is about life. In as far as it successfully depicts the struggles and triumphs of the human spirit, it is absolutely the result of my having been blessed with many joyful relationships. Please allow me a moment to recognize some of these people.

To my family, for the volumes of anecdotes that make for great storytelling and the love and compassion that you each offer in your own way, I am immensely proud and blessed to be included amongst you. I love you all.

To my many friends, both new and old, you challenge me, make me laugh, share my tears, and allow me to grow. Thank you for all that you are, and all that you do.

To those who critiqued the manuscript of this book including: Joanne, Kim, Mandy, Dale, Vera, Ian, Bruce, Cliff, Nancy, Domenic, Louise, Kevin, Deborah, Valerie, Glenn, Rick, Martin, Faith, Kathryn, Elaine, Trish, Graeme, Lynn, Karen, Bill, Pam, Tom, Russ and Paul, I owe my many thanks. The virtues of this work are attributed to you; the failings are completely my own.

To my editors at The Wyndham Press, Faith Nostbakken and Kim McLean-Fiander, I feel that praise alone for your contributions is insufficient. Your dedication to this project has been both inspirational and humbling. My hope is that the finished work is in some small way gratifying to you.

To Domenic Sallese for his artistic talents in the design of this book's cover, and Kevin Spreekmeester for his profound abilities as a photographer, I am grateful for your contributions, your friendship and your continued belief in this project.

To Paul Bates for your friendship, fellowship and corporate stewardship in creating healthy, ethical workplaces, I am inspired by your example. Thank you for your foreword to this book.

To Kim, for your continued belief, your attentive ear, your gentle spirit, and the wisdom of your counsel, I am eternally grateful. For me, you have always been what Wordsworth described as "a host of golden daffodils." I am filled with joy by your presence.

To each of my mentors in life including my mother, Ailsa Morris, my dad, Bob Fiander, and my good friend, Ian Blicq, this book is an extension of the legacy that you have left within me. I will always be grateful.

And to Joanne, my teacher, mentor, friend, critic, editor and partner in all matters of the heart and soul, I thank you for all that you are. You are my beloved of my soul.
God Bless you.

David McLean

Foreword

Corporate culture begins and ends in the corner office.

I was given the privilege of the title President for the first time roughly a decade and a half ago. However, I may have only truly come to understand the role of leadership in the last half-decade. Leadership begins with vision, and involves enabling, challenging, uplifting, and making room for others. Leadership is about exploring one's vulnerabilities in public, and it is about making one's office the safest place in the company. Above all, leadership is about ethics, accountability and authenticity, about recognizing when you're on the wrong path and getting back on the right one. C.S. Lewis wrote that, ironically, it is often the person who turns back to find where they took the wrong fork in the road who actually gets ahead the fastest.

Having been in a leadership role for half my working life, I can also tell you that it is impossible to work with human capital without understanding that there is something very profound going on; something spiritual. I have come to believe that it is spirituality that connects humans to one another. Yet, we somehow find it easier to email jokes to our colleagues than to explore this phenomenon. For me, this exploration has brought peace, reconciliation with my secular and temporal lives and, above all, a daily reminder of the need for ethics and integrity in the workplace.

It has been said that integrity is how we behave when others cannot see us; is there anything more fundamental than this? One of my children sent me an email recently to complain about feeling unappreciated in her workplace and, as I responded, I became horrified with the thought that a member of our company might one day send a similar note to their dad. Passion for ethics and for involvement is the genetic material we must build our companies with.

The Soul Café is a profound reminder that when these simple but challenging principles are not upheld, the fabric of trust is destroyed. It is also a wonderful example of two other phenomena: first, that people of principle are under an obligation to do the right thing; second, that there is such a thing as divine appointment, that is, of another person being placed in our lives for the explicit purpose of changing us, a concept that coincidentally occurs in a number of faiths.

As leaders, our most crucial task is straightforward, thank God. It is to provide leadership and, to paraphrase Nelson Mandela, let our light shine, which unconsciously will give other people permission to do the same.

Enjoy *The Soul Café*.

Paul Bates, *President & C.E.O., Charles Schwab Canada*

Prologue

A s we enter the 21st century, the prospect of the new millennium plays with our imagination. We find ourselves hoping that something profound will happen to improve our lives. Many of us find ourselves routinely questioning the status quo. In our professional lives, from the coffee rooms to the boardrooms, the conversations are familiar. How can the company expect me to give more, when I already feel like I'm performing on empty? Are there better ways of doing things? Can I be more efficient with my time? Why can't the organization do something to make me feel that they're listening? Why can't they acknowledge me? Why can't they bring joy into the workplace? Is joy in the workplace even possible, or am I asking too much? If the company expects to create leaders, why doesn't it teach by example? Why does everyone around here always seem to be so apathetic, so humorless? Where is the passion for work, for contributing as part of a team?

If that were all, our lives would be sufficiently tormented. But our personal interests, like our professional ones, have also been the cause of relentless examining and questioning. Too many of us have become enslaved by the daily routine of life, too tired to think, too numb to feel, until one day something causes us to stumble and fall down. Lying in a lump on the ground, we realize that although our physical self may be unscathed, our emotional being has become fractured. That brief ungraceful moment assessing ourselves releases emotions from the core of our being that threaten to engulf us with a deeper pain. We become immobilized by the realization that we no longer know who we are. Is this all there is to life? What happened to my dreams? What is my purpose? Why do I always feel anxious when I sit down at the end of the day? Why do I find now that even the best parts of my life often fail to excite me? What is my legacy?

These questions may sound familiar, but the answers never seem to follow, do they? Why is that? Why is it that seemingly straightforward questions about our humanity refuse to elicit straightforward answers? Perhaps life has become so distracted, dispassionate and anonymous that we have lost a sense of who we are and of who we want to become. We feel incomplete, less than whole. In our hectic world of job loss, burnout, stress, little league, vacuous TV trite, and instant everything, where our attention span has been reduced to the point where we burn the minute rice, we have sacrificed a piece of ourselves. Simply put, we have lost our souls. On the journey of recovery, we find that only by investing time and energy in ourselves and listening to our life-force, can we hope to uncover the answers that we seek and finally embrace the prospect of new soulful beginnings.

This book is a fictional account of one man's quest to understand a debilitating emptiness in a life rich with material comforts and to bravely strike out on a journey that may eventually lead him to peace, comfort and a feeling of wholeness. The plot is contrived, yet it speaks to the heart of all of us who have struggled within a world where society's elusive goals have become the focus of our existence. If what you seek is a prescription for peace of spirit that will serve you professionally and personally, then please pull up a comfortable chair, relax, and join us on our journey to *The Soul Café*.

Introductions

> *To be nobody but yourself in a world which is doing its best to make you like everybody else is to fight the hardest battle you can fight, but never stop fighting.*

e.e.cummings

Leaning back in my chair, I search the room for cues that will help me to remember the events of the past year. The dim light from the desk lamp is filtered through a nearby glass of wine, and a burgundy glow is cast across the picture-strewn walls of my home office. Neat stacks of paper occupy one corner of the workspace, while framed photographs of family and friends fill the other. Mellowed by two glasses of wine, I contemplate the task ahead of me. In the hopes of helping myself reconcile the events of the past year, my therapist has asked me to chronicle them. I fumble through my mind for a logical starting point, but as I have grown to appreciate, life is seldom rational and the thoughts are slow in coming. After several minutes of reverie induced by the pictures before me, a photograph of my son's hockey team dislodges my mental block, and a bittersweet memory teases out my story. The journey began in the early part of March, some nine months ago...

It had become a rare event for me to find time just for myself, but this morning, my wife Catherine had taken our son, Kyle, to hockey practice since they were having team pictures taken. Days before she had explained in a slightly chilling tone, "Four years Kyle's been in hockey and four pictures have been taken, and still there's not a single one where Kyle is smiling. I don't know what you say to him, but this time will be different. He'll smile for his mom." Funny. I thought that he held back the smile because he wanted to look tough. Whatever the reason, being able to sleep in and then read the paper without interruption was a treat that offset the little tirade I had to endure.

Picking up the Tribune, I flipped from one section to another until the Sports page was in full view. Dropping the rest of the paper on the kitchen floor, I began to devour one headline after another.

"Wow!" I thought to myself, " This guy must've lived a full life. A hundred and three years old and born in Montreal, too. Probably that winter air that helped to preserve him. Sixty years older than me. Six more decades of life, of experience.... Imagine all the good times, imagine the disappointments...." My eyes left the lengthy obituary of the accomplished architect who had left my adopted home of Chicago with such a profound legacy of sporting complexes, and continued to dart from page to page, digesting the words in front of me. Satisfied, I put down the paper for a moment, closed my eyes, and felt the heat of the morning sun struggle through the panes of the kitchen windows, and beat upon me. Although reasonably well-rested, I found myself with little energy and easily slipped away into a self-reflective trance. The house was still, and with its offer of peace, I was seduced to comply.

The thought of another sixty years of life visited my mind but rather than feeling in awe of the possibilities, I felt restless. My mind was like a bulletin board of meeting reminders, upcoming events, announcements, and, yes, even the featured menu offered by the office cafeteria, all garbled, all in chaos. Intermingled amongst this mental collage were commitments to my wife, son, father, and siblings. Each of these responsibilities sieged my mind, making it impossible to relax despite my solitude. No, another 60 years of mindless servitude was not for me.

Although the chair where I was sitting was comfortable, I felt that if I could just lie down for a few minutes I might manage to separate myself from these troubling thoughts long enough to relax. So, I left the kitchen and sought out the comfort of the sofa in the nearby living room. This room had been preserved in pristine condition in anticipation of potential visitors; however, few had tread across its plush ivory carpet. Fewer still had remarked on the classic elegance of its decor in the nine years we had lived here. It was like a museum gallery, distant and formal. If rooms could talk, this one would cry out for the emptiness that had started within it which had slowly metastasized throughout the house, and into the lives of its three inhabitants. Listless and apathetic to household norms, I collapsed on to the sofa, turned my head to feel the full effect of the morning sun, and tried to surrender my mental clutter.

I found myself slipping in and out of consciousness. After what seemed to be about half an hour I settled into that state of blissful ambivalence between asleep and awake where dreams come easily. My eyes were closed. I was quiet. My mind slowly opened up to a much earlier chapter in my life, a time of innocence, when I was a child in suburban Montreal.

I was born of French and Scottish parents in Dorval, Quebec, on a frigid day, the 15th of February, 1956. My mother, Elise Boucher, from a proud Quebecois family, often recounted the trip to the hospital and how difficult it was to determine whether she was out of breath due to the labor pains or the subzero temperatures. With a smile on her face and a chuckle in her voice she explained how she cursed my father for not pre-warming the car, for the bone-chilling temperature, for the icy roads, and for anything else she could think of that frosty winter morning. My father, Steven, was all-too familiar with the passionate vocabulary that could emerge from the mouth of his otherwise saintly wife when she was riled up. He maintained his good humor throughout the twelve-hour labor and was rewarded with a healthy baby boy, tipping the scales at nearly nine pounds. With brown curly hair and eyes to match, I, their first born, started life with countless comparisons made to the French-Canadian side of the family. Without hesitation, they called me Ian Philippe, to reflect the proud Scottish ancestry of my father and the colorful flamboyance of my mother's francophone heritage. A few months after my third birthday, I vaguely recall the arrival of my baby sister, Marie. Her vocal capacity at birth was to foreshadow what was in store for me over the next fifteen years! Our number as a family grew to five with the arrival of Shawn in August of 1961. And so it was that we three Archer children began our journey on this earth, blessed by two extraordinarily devoted parents.

Growing up near proud and historic Montreal in the late '50s and early '60s offered us a rare education in cultural blending. Virtually every aspect of the predominantly French speaking population's lives was seasoned by our Roman Catholic faith, including our food, work, and even family planning. Mom was the fourth of nine children, which at the time was considered an average brood for a Quebecois household. Yet despite its size, Mom's family, like so many others at the time, was held close together because of its faith, strong character, and warmth. In most French households, the mother was a central unifying figure, and this matriarchal tradition carried forward into the Archer home. Dad, a native of Princeton, New Jersey, found this to be in stark contrast to the family life he had experienced, but quickly accepted the French-Canadian culture as his own.

My father, Steven Archer, was a good and decent man having worn his hands in many trades by the time he was forty. When the demand for his craftsmanship in custom cabinetry slowed, he secured the family income by plumbing with a family friend. For a period, he also tried to earn a living at furniture making and, although incapable of competing with the speed of the large factories, his skill was evident in the beauty of each piece he wrought. It was obvious to all that Dad was passionate about his creations. You could see it in his face every time he showed his latest piece.

As was typical for the time, Mom didn't work outside the home after we kids arrived, but in many ways, her responsibilities surpassed those of my Dad. After all, in addition to managing all of the aspects of the home, Mom also was our tutor, our audience, and our moral authority for much of our impressionable years. And in our bilingual home, Mom had twice as many ways to articulate her love, compassion, devotion, annoyance and anger. Although she seldom found it within herself to express the latter, when occasion demanded, she brought new meaning to the phrase, "Hell hath no fury" . The unsuspecting soul who might have challenged her, usually ended up submissively performing some serious act of repentance. All the same, we knew that Mom and Dad's love for us was unconditional and always felt as if our home was a sanctuary where their love and respect enveloped us like a warm soft blanket right out of the dryer.

That was the case at least until the late '60s when our world was continuously threatened by a small group of radical Quebecois known as the Front de Liberation au Quebec or FLQ who sought a stage for their political agenda through indiscriminate acts of violence. By the summer of 1968, when the acrid stench of gunpowder in the air became too familiar to us all, in a decisive act of defiance against tyranny, we found our family embarking for a new home in the rolling countryside of Upper New York State.

Riiiiiiiing,Riiiiiiiinnnnnggg,Riiiiiiiinnnnngggg. The harsh sound of the phone jarred me from my state of bliss. I grabbed it before the fourth ring and listened as Catherine spoke,

"Hello Ian."

"Hello," I answered in a fog.

"Did I wake you? You sound tired."

"I just dozed off. I feel exhausted these days."

There was silence at the end of the phone, which I sensed was my wife's way of holding back some comment about me sleeping while she was busy with our son. I could feel the muscles in my neck tightening out of frustration.

"What's up?" I asked.

"I'm just stopping to pick up some milk for breakfast and was wondering whether we needed anything else."

"No, we're fine."

"Are you sure? Couldn't you just check the fridge?"

"We're fine," I answered abruptly.

"OK, I'll see you in ten minutes or so. G'bye."

"Bye."

After hanging up the phone, I glanced at the clock on the kitchen wall. An hour had passed since I laid down in the living room slipping in and out of that delicious state where it was safe to recount my humble beginnings. Now, fully awake, I found myself desperately trying to slip back. My mother's ability to evoke a feeling of contentment in me was unlike anything I had experienced in the past several years. I had always kept the smells, sounds, and emotions of my childhood closely guarded, protected against intruders. I seldom revisited these memories, for what purpose was served in revisiting the past? It was a different time, with different values, and simpler needs, I told myself. It was unrealistic to expect that I could find such a life now. Wasn't it?

As my reflections evaporated, I was left with a groggy mind, so I got up, walked to the powder room and splashed my face with water. Back to the reality of my life: It was Sunday, March 7th, 1999, and I had much to consider for the following day. Friday afternoon's memo had outlined the agenda for an executive meeting that would likely determine the fate of several staff, including two of my own who had claimed that several executives of the firm were guilty of fiscal, administrative and ethical improprieties. As Vice President of Corporate Development, a post which I'd held for the previous three years, I'd been asked to chair an investigative committee examining the allegations raised and to report back to the executive committee. It was obvious to me that my recommendations would decide the fate of both myself and others. I was anxious as I'd had only two weeks to review the information and felt inadequately versed to speak to the issues.

As I played out various scenarios in my head, I heard the garage door open and minutes later the sounds of Catherine and Kyle. Returning home from hockey practice, Kyle always had an impressive appetite, so I went into the kitchen to prepare Sunday brunch, a tradition learned from my father and one I had continued to honor. Catherine, my spouse of 13 years, found me with a frying pan in hand.

"Good morning," she said defiantly as she passed me in the kitchen. "Did you have a good sleep?"

I felt the bite in her tone, but decided against an argument. "Yes," was all I could muster up, then continued making breakfast. Although I wished for a more peaceful atmosphere in the house, it seemed that Catherine and I were more at each other lately. Perhaps we could make it through breakfast without incident.

Pancakes, sausage, orange juice, coffee and cereal were on the menu today, and as the food approached readiness and cast off its delicious aroma, Kyle's yells of approval could be heard from his bedroom upstairs. In nanoseconds he was downstairs, freshly showered, dressed, and ready to eat.

As usual, Kyle gave his Mom a quick kiss on the cheek and turned to me with arms outstretched. Wearing the greasy smells of sausage and pancakes, I embraced my son and it occurred to me that this was the best part of my day. As I pushed the last few sausages around in the frying pan amidst splattering fat, I realized that my life had become validated by this single, simple act. Not even the occasional gentle touch from my wife could stir me from the numbing trite of my life anymore. This fact stunned me. Shaking off this feeling of dread, I poured myself a cup of coffee, sat down, and tried to escape into Sunday brunch with my family.

In no time flat, Kyle gratefully inhaled a plate of pancakes, sausages drenched in maple syrup, and was now pouring a bowl of cereal. Catherine, on the other hand, had a look that suggested she had some less charitable comment to make about breakfast.

"What is it?" I asked, tempting fate.

"I just thought we were going to have eggs this morning."

Sheepishly, I confessed, "We only had two eggs left. Sorry."

Catherine didn't need to speak. Her 'I told you so' look

was sufficient to make me feel apologetic for being so curt with her on the phone earlier.

Kyle broke the silence. "Good breakfast, Dad," he remarked as he rose to find the milk.

Incredulously, I asked, "Where's it all going, bud?"

"I'm growing. I'm only five-foot-three. Terry Conners, on our team is only two months older than me, and he's five-foot-four," he stated in defense.

Twelve-years-old and already five-foot-three. My little boy. I was sure he'd surpass my height of five-eleven. Looking at him as he dug through the refrigerator for milk, I thought about the nine years that we had lived in that house. We measured Kyle each year against the back door to chart his growth. Four years ago, he had asked, "When will I be old enough to drive?" I took him to the door and marked five-foot-eight in black marker thinking he would be sixteen by that height. At this rate, however, I was going to have a fourteen-year-old behind the wheel! It was thoughts like this that caused the gray in my hair. Kyle returned to the table having recovered some day-old donuts along with the milk. Catherine and I stared in amazement at the spectacle before us. Sensing our amusement and always anxious to entertain, Kyle smiled like the Cheshire cat.

Between bites of donut, a half-garbled phrase emerged, "Are you still up to playing a little catch today, Dad?"

I remembered I'd promised Kyle that, weather permitting, I'd help him with his pitching. Although it was only early March and baseball season lay months away, he loved the game as much as hockey and wanted to improve before the season started. Despite all of the work issues on my mind, I found myself smiling and telling my son I would take him down to the diamond in an hour or two. I couldn't change my mind now. I firmly believed that a promise was not to be broken. When I made a promise, one could bet the farm that I would follow through. My promise was oak; it was my integrity and meant everything to me.

Catherine rose from the table and suggested Kyle finish his reading assignment before running off to play baseball. Compliantly, he wiped the milk from his mouth and darted upstairs. Catherine shared a glance with me as she cleaned the table and rebuked my offer of assistance with a gentle smile and a kiss on the head. It seemed that the humor of Kyle's antics allowed her to either forget or forgive my earlier shortcomings.

"I think you have more important things to do, Ian, but thanks anyway."

Of course, she was right.

About to enter into my office, I stopped for a moment to admire the view outside. Due to the unseasonably warm temperatures over the past week, the only trace of snow to be found lay cowering under our shady evergreens. The grass was brown, but with the sun offering up temperatures near 50 degrees, it would soon green up. The birds and squirrels released a chorus of sounds, and were accompanied by the harmonies of trickling water from the brook that dissected the back corner of our lot. The image excited my senses and seemed to hold great promise for the day.

In stark contrast to this scene, I found my office dark and foreboding. Within minutes I felt a pain between my eyes as I read the accusations, notes and testimony of the two managers under my charge who had launched this inquiry. Until recently, I had always taken pride in my ability to develop a strong team atmosphere that was open, flexible, and respectful. Trust was a hallmark of my department and its staff. It thus came as a shock to me shortly after Christmas vacation when I found myself facing one of my most seasoned project managers distraught over what he claimed was a complete lack of trust in the organization.

Paul Scott had been with Medicon for eleven years, eight of which had been working with me. When I was promoted to Vice President, Corporate Development six years ago, overseeing business development, public affairs and government affairs, Paul was a candidate for my former position, Director of Business Development. He was understandably upset when the position was offered to an outsider. Feeling that his skill in diplomacy could be better directed within our public affairs department, I told him I'd keep him top of mind when an opportunity presented itself. To help lessen the blow, I also took Paul out for drinks with a group of colleagues that night, sent him to a conference in Monterey, California, and gave him two days off with pay, encouraging him to take his family to the local amusement park at the company's expense. These were small personal gestures, I realize, but they spoke of the considerable respect I had for his valuable contributions to the company. Also, I hoped that they would help to dignify the pain of his rejection. In fact, he later told me that when offered a better position with a competitor six months later, he declined the offer because of the way he had been treated at Medicon.

As expected, Paul worked diligently that next year and, as I had hoped, a senior management post emerged within the public affairs department, for which Paul competed successfully. His ability to research potentially volatile issues and to develop strategies that resulted in improved relations with our customers was inspiring. Ironically, it was while doing what he became noted for that he uncovered evidence of a series of policy violations that had been concealed by at least one Vice President and by none other than Harold Stoner, Medicon's President and Chief Executive Officer. Amongst his allegations were expense account abuses and charges of harassment by several staff. When Paul contacted his usual network of internal officers for information that would help to explain the inconsistencies, he was suddenly stonewalled. His intuitive nature led him to conclude that there was a foundation for the charges and he strengthened his resolve to determine the veracity of the complaints. His tenacity was famous and his passion to uncover the truth was contagious. It was these traits that attracted a following of co-investigators throughout the firm. However, as additional information was gathered and senior executives implicated, the momentum dwindled until only Paul and a financial analyst, Karen MacDonald, remained on the case.

In my nine years with Medicon, I could count on my fingers how many times I had actually spoken with Karen. Despite that, I had been aware that she was hired about six years earlier, directly out of business school. I understood that she had been married briefly, then widowed after her husband was killed in a motorcycle accident. Her outgoing personality was lost as a result of the tragedy, and since then she had kept fairly reclusive, finding comfort alone or in the company of a few close friends. She worked within the finance department of the firm where she was hidden within a maze of cubicles. Professionally, by all accounts, she was a star. In fact, four years ago, she discovered a weak point in a firm with which Medicon was about to form an alliance. Her advice resulted in a restructuring of the contract, a piece of work which was not warmly received at the time by either party, but as history bore out, saved Medicon several million dollars in potential exposure when the other firm applied for Chapter 11 bankruptcy protection. I was the project director responsible for that alliance, and despite my initial misgivings about having a numbers person on the project, I later realized that Karen Macdonald saved my bacon. Personally, that experience awakened me to my own fallibility and limitations. Other executives at Medicon could recite similar near mishaps, but usually their inflated egos and personal insecurities prevented the words from being uttered except to close associates, and even then only when accompanied by the stench of cigar smoke and by breath heavy laden with scotch. I include myself within this group, for like my colleagues, I never had the courage to actually thank Karen for her help. Knowing her track record, however, I was both pleased and surprised that Paul had managed to adopt such a capable colleague to work on an internal project that was destined to be anything but safe and insular. I was confident that she would work well within the culture that I had tried to create amongst the people in my department.

Now, I had always tried to lead my staff in a manner that showed my humanity. I was fair, or at least I considered myself to be so, and by example had tried to develop teams that honored each other. Through truthfulness I had hoped to establish a trusting workplace. I believed my own integrity and ethics should be forged out of the strongest principles so that when held up to my staff they mirrored what I expected in their conduct. These things in mind, I encouraged my staff to work independently to a large measure, requesting only that they inform me should other executives from the firm become involved in a project. It was particularly troubling, therefore, when in the midst of contemplating a new strategic alliance, that I should be interrupted by a call from an irate Vice President of Sales, Tod Slater. Tod was phoning to complain about an overzealous staff member of mine who was probing relentlessly into expense files and performance appraisal records submitted by field managers. Peppering his remarks with a few choice expletives, Tod was otherwise very succinct and insisted I take appropriate action. Caught completely unaware, I found myself still digesting my good morning greeting to him when the phone disengaged. Rather than react too hastily, I had allowed myself to return to the task from which I had just been pried, content to speak with Paul after the regular 2:00 p.m. Thursday afternoon staff meeting.

At 3:45 p.m. that day, with the lengthy agenda concluded, I thanked everyone for their contributions and signaled for Paul to remain as a dozen of Medicon's best managers left the room. When asked about the incident, Paul explained that for the previous two-month period he and Karen had been carefully and systematically interviewing various staff and reviewing financial records to understand the nature of the issue and to ascertain whether there were any legitimate public sensitivities that should be considered. As they encountered resistance from staff, their suspicions grew and they resorted to more convoluted, yet equally effective, means of gathering the data. Paul and Karen had concealed their progress from me partially because they wanted to wash all conjecture from their analysis before presenting it to me and partially because they wanted to determine how I would react when one of my fellow executives insisted that they stop. I was a control group of one. Would I remain loyal to my staff or to the executive team? Although they were much more diplomatic in presenting the situation to me, in essence, that was their question. Paul finished his comments by presenting me with an interim report which, although brief, grabbed my interest. I found it impossible to put down.

Karen and Paul had also requested that Karen be transferred to my department to work on the project due to presumed misgivings amongst the finance department over Karen's current preoccupation. The requests seemed reasonable, so I phoned her boss immediately to propose a move. The reaction was surprising, suggestive of relief rather than annoyance, and so the paperwork was expedited to enable Karen to join my team by November 12th.

Although both Paul and Karen requested that I remain neutral throughout the investigation and therefore ill-informed, I insisted on bi-weekly updates of a general nature and that I be apprised in advance of any further potential backlash from the executive. They gave me their assurances and continued their work.

The weeks that followed prior to the Christmas break of 1998 should have foreshadowed for me the circumstances and decisions that I would have to face in the coming year. Perhaps I was caught up in the Christmas revelry that became far too frequent when enjoying executive privilege in a successful medical company. Perhaps I was too busy grasping for the proverbial brass ring, focussed on the outside world while slowly suffocating on the inside. Whatever the case, on that early January morning, when confronted by my good friend Paul who spoke passionately about the lack of trust at Medicon, my world began to crumble.

Too distracted by the white noise of the office environment, I had asked Paul to step out that afternoon to join me for a coffee at a nearby cafe. I had noticed this new place for a few months, but never had the occasion to visit until then. Its sign was bland compared to the rainbow of neon on the surrounding businesses. In fact, as I think about it now, I still can't remember its name. When we pulled up in front of the building, I found its exterior of salmon stucco to be unpretentious, a stark contrast to the hair salons and gift boutiques that flanked it on either side. It was a little oasis in a desert of trendy shops and exotic aesthetics. The chairs inside were plush and comfortable and soaked in soothing rich colors of blue, burgundy, green, and fawn, complementing the rich tones that adorned the walls and floor. Instrumental music played softly in the background and invited visitors to relax. Paul and I were not alone in this place, despite the time, so we settled into two large chairs in a quiet corner and ordered our coffee. After being served, I invited Paul to share his thoughts with me—candidly. He began by recounting his findings to date and explained how frustrated both he and Karen had been by the company-wide silence, deceit, and cover-up that had faced them at every turn. They were meticulous in their documentation and had begun to piece together a puzzle involving numerous sales representatives, managers, and directors falsifying company expense reports, making fraudulent personal claims, and harassing employees who threatened to expose the improprieties. Several female managers and representatives had also been dismissed over a one-year period and, when contacted by Karen or Paul, described incidences that involved both sexual and professional harassment. To date, six managers, two directors and one Vice President, namely Tod Slater, had been directly implicated and there were suggestions that the President, too, may have been aware of several of the policy violations described.

Whether aided by the soothing surroundings or by the warmth of the coffee on a cold winter day, I was reflective, and empathetic to Paul's concerns. Years of experience have taught me that when an organization abandons truth, trust becomes malnourished and soon perishes. Without trust, energy that could be used for productive behavior is consumed by contemplation and trepidation. Paul and Karen, two talented and committed employees who had given much of themselves to Medicon's success, had looked to their colleagues for answers and found only fear and denial.

The day after Paul's and my café conversation, I had met privately with both him and Karen and commissioned them to create an investigative team of five to establish conclusively who was involved in the improprieties, the charges being made, the impact of these actions, and the recommendations that could be made for the future. I had asked that the final report be submitted to me by the second week of February.

It was this fifty-page document, accompanied by testimonials, financial reports, other evidence and committee minutes that now, on this Sunday afternoon in March, littered my home office desk. My mind was agitated. After investing nine years with Medicon, what was my future there? Did I really want to stay on with a firm where such a poison could taint so many? Where was the leadership? What was the future of my team, especially if I were to speak out? Questions plagued my mind for answers, yet found none. I raised my head and noticed the time. I did not yet have the answers, but I was clear on one thing: I had a promise to keep. It was time to play catch with Kyle.

Lessons of Childhood

> *This above all, to thine ownself be true,*
> *And it must follow as the night, the day,*
> *Thou canst not then be false to any man.*

William Shakespeare

I found my son outside throwing a baseball up in the air and catching it, obviously anxious for me to appear. He had already grabbed my glove, so we jumped into the car and headed towards Deerborne's recreational park. The sky, bleached pale blue by the intensity of the sun, cast a surreal backdrop for the dozens of swallows, robins, ducks and geese that flew overhead. Although premature, it had the makings of a perfect Spring day.

Kyle ascended the pitching mound and I hovered over home plate, anxious to turn my thoughts away from the hours of contemplation that had burdened my mind earlier.

"OK, now Kyle, don't overdo it. Just throw a couple of easy pitches to me. Don't worry about your form, just concentrate on reaching home plate," I said.

The speed of the ball stung my hand through the glove and suddenly I felt very old. Perhaps Kyle was just trying to impress me.

"Hey, that was great, but remember accuracy is just as important. Concentrate on your target."

"You got it, Dad," he shouted eagerly.

Again, a thundering pitch, and again, right on the money. Time after time, my twelve- year-old listened to my coaching and responded with success. With each pitch came greater confidence and performance than the one before. Although I'm sure Kyle could have gone on much longer, after ninety minutes of catching, I was ready for a break.

"Super pitching, Kyle. You've improved a lot over last year."

"Thanks, Dad. I wanna be ready for try-outs this year. I really wanna be the starting pitcher."

"What? Are you kidding? With that arm of yours they'll be scouting you for the majors any day now!"

As we walked toward the car together, I asked, "Hey, would you like to grab a hot chocolate?"

"Sure, that would be great," Kyle said as I stored the baseball and gloves in the trunk.

We decided to walk rather than drive to a nearby mall where a popular coffee franchise could be found. As we started out, the lingering scent of the leather glove in my hand coupled with the bond of father and son led me back to a memorable time in my youth.

After graduating from Pembrook County High, about thirty minutes away from Syracuse, New York, I decided to return to Montreal to study science at McGill University. The opportunity to work in a research laboratory over the summer months provided me with the edge I needed at graduation to land my first job. Three offers presented themselves at the time — two in Palo Alto, California, working in research laboratories within newly developed biotechnology firms, and a third in a laboratory in Boston at Massachusetts General Hospital. Being young and adventurous, I opted to work in Palo Alto at a firm called Bionexus. Success there translated to an inside sales position. I soon sought greater responsibilities and the opportunity to travel, so left after three years to join Medica Domina, a boutique medical device firm, where I managed my first sales territory. I found that my university degree in biochemistry appealed to the technical audience who bought the firm's products and consequently I enjoyed early success in my sales career. As I became better established and more confident, I began to take a series of management courses, some offered by the company, some through the University of California at Berkeley. Their appeal to me was largely because I was able to apply what I had learned right away in my work. One day my district manager, Terry Winters, invited me to lunch on a perfect California summer afternoon to discuss my career. He suggested that my future at Medica Domina, or

MD as the firm was commonly known, was promising. Middle management was apparently already noticing my contributions to the company and saw particular merit in my extra-curricular academic pursuits. Terry advised that to progress in my career, I should return to school to obtain a business degree. With the brashness of youth, I drove to the Stanford campus later that afternoon to pick up the necessary application forms.

"Hey, Dad, check out that bodacious car! Sweet, huh?"

"What's that? Sorry, Kyle, what did you say?"

"The car, Dad, look at that red sports car."

During our walk we passed through a fairly affluent neighborhood where Kyle's attention was drawn to a bright red convertible proudly displayed in the horseshoe drive in front of its owner's home. I surmised that the silver-haired woman hovering over the vintage car was in fact its owner by the way she meticulously polished its chrome adornments.

"It looks to be about a '57 or '58 Corvette, Kyle. Pretty hot, isn't it?"

"Yeah. I'd like a car like that when I get my license."

It was the second time today that my thoughts had included the prospect of Kyle driving. I was not ready to consider that scenario and felt compelled to change the subject for my own sanity.

"Well, that's still a long way off. Maybe we could look into a new set of inline skates instead? By the way, where did "bodacious" come from?"

"I heard it in a movie, and it sounds cool. The kids in my class use it all the time."

"That's very cool," I said with a smile.

Kyle returned the smile as we continued on our walk. Seconds later I found my mind taking me back to the days at Stanford when I met Catherine.

Although late in the registration process, I applied to Stanford's MBA program. The tuition, though prohibitively expensive for me, was brought within reach through the generous assistance of Medica Domina, who I presumed had seen in me both management potential and an opportunity to promote the company to key medical staff at Stanford. MD also extended a partial leave from most of my duties at the company so I could complete my studies while maintaining certain administrative sales functions. Due to my evolving responsibilities at MD over the two years that followed, I was given the chance to both study and earn a reasonable income simultaneously, which at that point in my life was important as I had no intention of compromising my financial status.

My MBA progressed well, despite the workload, and time passed quickly. Without warning, my new college friends soon began talking of summer employment plans and second-year electives and, shortly afterwards, I found myself returning to campus for my second and final year at Stanford. It was that fall that I met Catherine Torres, a third-year Political Science major. She was busy canvassing students for their opinions on the Republicans' recently publicized foreign affairs platform, when she stopped me on my way to a Human Resource Management class. When I showed little interest in the Republican platform, she became enraged and resolved to educate me on the significance of the issues. Whether it was the enjoyment I got out of listening to her obvious political savvy or from admiring the delicate curves of her petite frame, I felt compelled to ask her to dinner. It is now sobering to realize how an apparently innocuous moment in our past can later define a great part of our life. This was certainly the case that October in 1984 when, with a coyish giggle, this intelligent, attractive, ebony haired, twenty-one year-old woman said yes to my dinner invitation.

I remember well how we laughed together and how we were both so passionate about life. Catherine shared with me fairly intimate details about her family, including that her father, Miles Torres, a rather famous criminal attorney, overdrank and underachieved as a father and husband. She resented him for allowing his career to consume his life. It was equally clear that she was not impressed with the dutiful and complacent role her mother had assumed to preserve appearances. An only child, Catherine admitted that an emotional distance had wedged itself between her parents and herself, a distance that had become more pronounced over the last few years that she lived in Northern California, while they remained in Miami.

Believe it or not, on that first evening together, over pasta and Cabernet, I realized that Catherine Torres was everything I could imagine in a wife. She was slower in reciprocating my feelings, but nonetheless

*by the end of the school year, with my degree com-
plete, we became engaged. And just two weeks after
her Class of '86 ascended the stage, we found ourselves ascending the altar in a small Catholic church
in Palo Alto and beginning our life together as husband and wife.*

*The two years following my graduation had me
rapidly promoted at MD from sales representative
to sales manager and then on to marketing management. The firm was doing well and had recuperated
its investment in me many times over, largely
through my introducing key Stanford physicians to
MD's new line of diagnostic products. Catherine
quickly landed a position as an associate consultant
within a large independent practice of management
consultants. In our first year of married life, I especially remember the brilliant repartee of school
friends and business colleagues we hosted in our
home, as well as the long talks that Catherine and I
both enjoyed as we walked the coastline or hiked
the forested hills of Northern California. There were
always exciting things to do and see and I was often
moved by Catherine's passion for life. In this respect
she reminded me of my mother. Then, when we
thought life couldn't be more fulfilling, along came
our son. Our beautiful...*

"Oh, gross! Roadkill."

"What? Oh, that. The poor thing. I guess it was trying
to make its way back into the woods," I surmised while trying to rationalize the plight of the raccoon that lay about 10
feet in front of Kyle and me on the road.

Picking up a stick from the wooded area beside us, Kyle headed to the road. His intentions were clear.

"I want to put him back in his home," he said, with compassion in his face.

"OK, after the green truck goes by."

Then off we went, carefully sliding the limp body to the curb, then up over the sidewalk until it found a resting place in the wet ditch beside us. Kyle tossed the stick, then turned to me and found my approving glance. He always had been compassionate and caring. I admired him for those qualities.

I placed my arm over his shoulder and drew him close to me for a moment, then continued on our walk.

Together, Catherine and I conjectured as to exactly when and where Kyle was conceived. Perhaps it was following an intimate evening of fine food and wine accompanied by the mellow notes of Miles Davis. Such evenings always seemed to end with our eager bodies in a passionate embrace, casting a kaleidoscope of shadows on the candlelit walls of our bedroom. On the other hand, it may have been while camping in the northern hills where I would feel helpless to the captivating beauty of the setting sun reflecting upon the face of my bride. I suppose the precise time or coordinates are irrelevant. The feelings we shared were not, though. As was the case with many of my memories of youth, the thoughts of those early years of marital passion had also been archived in some remote, undisturbed part of my mind. What I did remember was the shock we both experienced when Catherine announced she was pregnant. Although we had both planned to have children one day, we were caught unaware that "one day" would be so soon. Suddenly, we were overwhelmed with preparations. Soon, we were welcoming houseguests who wished to share in this exciting time in our lives. Mom and Dad arrived one week before the baby's arrival and my sister Marie, a single, twenty-eight year-old insurance salesperson, arrived from Salt Lake City two days later. Shawn, my baby brother, was twenty-six and deeply engrossed in research for a PhD in plant physiology at Ohio State and so was unable to join us. As wonderful as it felt for me to be with the family again, Catherine was not in good humor and I continuously found myself in the middle of family disagreements. The birth of our son, Kyle Thomas Archer, helped to put Catherine at ease and reminded us all, at least for a brief time, of our own vulnerability and of the beauty of a loving, caring family.

"Hey, Dad, are we close yet?"

"Huh?"

"Are we close to the hot chocolate place yet?"

Sensing his irritation, I replied apologetically, "I'm sorry for being so unattentive Kyle. I've had a lot on my mind lately. It's right across the street there—the orangey-brown looking place." I felt my explanation was overused, but reasoned that I couldn't get into my issues with my son, so it would have to do.

"It's OK, Dad. Thanks for playing catch with me. It was fun."

"No problemo, bud. I had fun too."

The aromas that wafted through the air as we approached the coffee house refreshed me. I knew Kyle was aware of my mental distraction during our walk and that he was feeling awkward despite my explanation. I placed my hand on his head and we shared a smile. As we entered the café it was obvious that the nice weather had enticed others out of their winter lairs. The place was packed. As Kyle scouted out a table for us, I stood in line to order our hot chocolates. The glass display case, reserved for delectable creations such as fudge brownies, huge cookies, tortes and muffins, was too inviting to pass up, so by the time I was ready to order, I asked for two cookies as well as our drinks. Navigating with the tray to our table, I could see Kyle's approval at first sight of the cookies. All had been forgiven.

"So," I began, as we enjoyed our snack, "how's school?"

Although the question was overused, Kyle knew that I had asked out of genuine interest.

"OK! I got 92% on last week's math test and an "A" on my science report. Oh yeah, and some teachers from Deerborne Academy visited us and said I could join the karate club and the swimming team and, if I am big enough by grade nine, then I could try out for the football team too."

"Is that right?" I said supportively, not wanting to burst any bubbles prematurely. "Which one interests you most?" Of course, I knew the answer in advance.

Kyle stated confidently, "All of them."

In addition to having a great academic program, Deerborne Academy, a private co-ed school for grades 7 - 12, was also reputed for its enviable list of sporting activities. Catherine and I had discussed the idea of sending Kyle there the following year since many of his friends from the neighborhood would be attending. Judging by Kyle's enthusiasm, any debate on the subject would clearly have been moot.

"So you think you would like it at Deerborne, do you?" I asked.

"Uh-huh, and everyone else is going there, too," he added. " One of the teachers said the students can try out for plays starting in seventh grade."

This was the first I had heard Kyle express any interest in drama, so I probed deeper, "Would you like to try out for a play?"

"Of course I would," Kyle responded. "Do you remember Mr. Tyler, my teacher from last year?"

Before I could offer my confirmation, Kyle continued, "Well, he's directing our Spring play, and I'm playing this man who's a shop keeper and Mr. Tyler says I'm great because I remember my lines and have lots of enthusiasm."

That was not hard to believe, but I didn't remember ever hearing about Kyle's stage debut before. Perhaps it had just slipped his mind. Nonetheless, it brought back to mind my own debut in Hamlet, playing the role of Polonius, advisor to the Danish court, in my senior high-school year. Though Polonius is usually thought of as a complete fool in the play, the words he offers up to his son, Laertes, upon the young man's departure, stick with me still, " Neither a borrower, nor a lender be... this above all, to thine ownself be true...." The words echoed in my ears as Kyle and I departed on our return to the car. "To thine ownself be true." "To thine ownself be true." It was as if some apparition was guiding me to a renewed understanding of these words, and I was comforted.

"Dinner will be ready by six tonight," Catherine volunteered as her ball players entered the house.

"Thanks, I'll be in my study until then," I informed her, and left the details of our afternoon to be recounted to her through the words of our son. I sunk into my leather office chair and soon became contemplative of the afternoon's events. I thought about how my own father used opportunities such as an afternoon catch session or working over the engine of our car to share his wisdom with me. When I left home for university, Dad, while bent over a sawhorse making a mahogany china cabinet, offered some advice that has remained with me ever since. He said, "Know who you are, son, and what you want. The rest will follow as it's supposed to." Though I have heard many eloquent speeches offered by great leaders over the twenty-five years since, none has been more profound or more accessible to me than those simple words my Dad shared that day. Like the beautiful piece of furniture he crafted that has served both his home and mine so well over the years, so have his words stood the test of time serving to remind me of his wisdom.

But thoughts of my dad were incomplete without also remembering the teachings of my mother. Mom was always so strong, with an inimitable passion for life even when diagnosed with breast cancer seven years ago. She expressed greater concern for family than for herself, but then for her, she and family were one. She often shared with those closest to her that dad was her soulmate, guided into her life by some divine spirit. To her, the family that they had created together were extensions of their own souls. This was obvious to me, for whenever I was with her and the family I felt an inner peace and fulfillment like no other time. This feeling dwindled after I moved away and has evaded me entirely since mom died three and a half years ago in the fall of '95.

I felt hopeless at the time. I worked for a leading firm in the field of cancer diagnostics and yet had failed to be of any help to my own mother suffering from this inhumane disease. But I was comforted when in the quiet repose of the last few months of her life, she repeated a passage she had composed many years earlier...

"You're an Archer, my son. Hold your bow with integrity and let your thoughts be true and they will find their mark and success will find you."

So often I had heard those words as a young adult and so often they had cured me of my pains and given me confidence and direction.

Mother was not here for me now, and my memory of her was a poor surrogate. As I sat alone in my dim office on this Sunday afternoon contemplating my work and my life, tears welled up in my eyes. I felt betrayed, and yet I didn't know by whom. I was a successful businessman. I'd gone to school, worked hard, married my sweetheart, and had a wonderful family. I was a pretty good father and a faithful husband. Yet, here I was feeling like I'd been kicked and beaten 'till the wind had been knocked from my lungs. Life wasn't supposed to be like this. Something was devouring me from the inside. I felt hollow and lost.

Time passed. I wiped my eyes in the realization that dwelling on my losses wasn't helping me to prepare for the challenges I faced at work in the coming week. I knew that I must have more time to resolve the issues at hand, and so decided to ask for just that the following day.

Doing the Wrong Thing for the Right Reasons

A good heart can no more be concealed than a bad one.

Frank Vizarre

I slept peacefully that night, probably because of my mental fatigue and the fresh air and exercise I got while playing with Kyle. But Catherine's sensitivity towards my emotional turmoil also helped. Reminiscent of the early years of our marriage, she had prepared our bedroom with aromatic candles and soothing music while I soaked myself in a warm and relaxing tub. After bathing, Catherine entreated me to join her in the bedroom, where she thoughtfully gave me a massage to help rid my body of the toxins that all my stress had deposited. Later, we made love and embraced a deep restorative sleep.

The following morning I awoke prematurely to a darkened room that still held the scent of vanilla. I knew I should have felt content, but instead I was agitated. It was twenty minutes before my alarm was due to go off so I lay still, thinking about the previous day and specifically about my relationship with Catherine. Within a single day our interactions could swing from being positive to negative and back again. At one point, we could be arguing about something completely trivial and feel angered and hurt. During these moments, I tended to retreat inside myself and be aloof when answering her, waiting for the opportunity to escape from her verbal confrontation. Later, we could be found showing considerable compassion and concern for one another. At those times, I felt closer to no one. I wondered what had happened to my relationship with Catherine. Although I knew that we loved one another and that we were intimate with some regularity, the passion and energy that we once shared seemed to have dissipated. Searching for answers, I again found myself in the past!

The three years that followed Kyle's birth were as one would expect. In a word—hectic. Feeling isolated from the pulse of city life, Catherine returned to work six months after Kyle was born. Blessed to have found a wonderful Spanish woman by the name of Anna in whose hands we could entrust the care of our son, we rarely suffered from serious separation anxiety. We took great pains to orchestrate our busy professional schedules so that at least one of us could be with Kyle for a part of each day. It was clear to those closest to us that our new family unit was central to our lives. Catherine and I believed we shared similar values and we both professed a strong faith. However, this was seldom tested and therefore, in practice, was subliminal or implied. Now, years later, the wisdom of experience has suggested to me that at some point in those first few years of marriage and parenthood we had developed fear in being openly vulnerable with one other, incapacitating us from a deeper exploration of our values and ourselves. We nonetheless believed we were principled people and these principles formed the foundation of our home life. From the beginning of our life together, I sought to emulate the soulfulness of my childhood home, while Catherine sought simply to ensure a better environment than that which she remembered as a child.

We both grew professionally during those years, with financial success a companion to our long hours. Much of the life Catherine and I had treasured before Kyle's arrival, such as hiking in the hills or having dinner parties with our friends, had to be sacrificed out of simple recognition that there wasn't the time. We tended to make up for these deficiencies by aggressively pursuing the next step on our respective corporate ladders and by spending our disposable income on expensive clothes, jewelry, home improvements and furnishings. For a time, we also developed a fascination for West Coast art, particularly paintings depicting the unique geography and cultural influences found in the Northern California region. As the intoxicating spending continued, however, its capacity to serve as a substitute for our happiness lessened.

Around this time, a former colleague from Stanford told me about a senior position he was trying to fill for a large medical manufacturer, called Medicon. The post was Director of Business Development located in their sparkling new head office on the outskirts of Chicago. Chicago—-home to the Cubs, the Bears, the Black Hawks and the Bulls. Home to deep-dish pizza and Oprah and birthplace of the wind. I reasoned that a little investigative work into Medicon couldn't hurt despite my confidence that Catherine would never consider moving from the life that we had built in Palo Alto.

After tenaciously analyzing the firm over the weeks that followed, I discovered that Medicon was an established entity involved in researching, developing, manufacturing and marketing a wide range of medical products including a promising new line of diagnostic products for breast and colorectal cancer. Its financial situation was very sound and the management was regarded by others in the industry as being notably ethical. The opportunity to direct a team of professionals in the acquisition of new products and technologies was the challenge I was seeking. In fact, the more I thought about applying for the position, the more I felt it would sweep away the feelings of insufficiency I had found increasingly clouding my mind at that time. I still had to speak with Catherine on the matter, though, and I knew that would not be an easy discussion.

She had left her parents and Miami to build a life for herself, independent of them and their influence. So much so in fact that, contrary to my advice, she didn't contact her parents about Kyle until after he was born. An opportunity to bring the Torres family closer together was turned into one which offended the parents instead. But Catherine argued bitterly in defense of her actions and, to preserve family peace, I allowed her this victory. To further her case for remaining in California, she reminded me of the support system we had established for Kyle, the friends we had made, and the home we had created. Despite her persuasive arguments, she could see in my face that I needed this change. At points in our discussions, it was clear that she too was ready for a change from the status quo. Ultimately, the decision was made together to apply, and three months later, the decision was made together to accept Medicon's offer.

Shortly after accepting the job, Catherine and I took a week to scout several suburban neighborhoods surrounding Chicago before settling on Deerborne, a heavily wooded, upper-middle-class community of professionals who demanded convenient services, excellent schools and medical care, and a superior quality of life. With the strong California housing market in 1990, our home in Palo Alto had appreciated several times its original purchase price, enabling us to acquire a large two-story Colonial style home on an expansive treed lot without a mortgage. Due to our improved financial situation, Catherine was content to stay with three-year-old Kyle at home for several months before seeking outside work. The pleasure of finding our new home was coupled with a feeling of independence leaving us both exhilarated.

The move was an emotional one, leaving behind many memories, friends, and a way of life. As the airport taxi pulled away from our California home, Catherine appeared stoic.

"It's time for a new chapter, boys," she began, as Kyle and I looked on. "Change can be good. It will be good. New friends, new possibilities." As she spoke, she sought reassurance in my eyes.

"Absolutely," I said. "It's going to be great."

I mentally scrolled through that time in our lives as I lay in a semi-conscious state, aware that my forecast for our lives upon departure from California was rather ambitious, but equally aware that my alarm would sound at any moment. I opened my eyes and, with my face in my hands, tried to rub away the fatigue. Nine years had passed since we had left California. Some of our promises to one another had been met, some not. Quiet times between Catherine and me reading or holding or talking about our most guarded secrets had been lost. We dismissed these omissions from our lives as casualties of our schedules. Catherine's consulting career had always demanded her complete attention and had often been the cause of missed dinners and fractured weekends. Likewise, my schedule had me travelling about the country two to three times a month. The challenges at Medicon over the years provided a poor excuse for the many moments stolen from my family. Whatever time was left had us rushing to prepare meals or shopping or driving Kyle here or there. Seldom did we have the energy to engage ourselves in deeply spiritual discussions. In that respect, I rationalized, we were like the majority. So, I convinced myself that it was OK that who I was as a person both at home and work had become foreign to me. And Catherine convinced herself that more time together would be good, but unrealistic. And so we passed off our own inadequacies and the consequences of them to Life and returned to our regularly pre-programmed days. I opened my eyes with a feeling of anxiousness. It was time to get up.

The loud obnoxious beeping of the alarm had me out of bed in seconds. After showering, I got dressed, and then woke Kyle and went downstairs for breakfast. Catherine joined me moments later and we exchanged a familiar glance and smile. As the coffee perked and spread its delicious aroma throughout the kitchen, Catherine busily prepared Kyle's lunch, while I broke with the routine and made French toast for everyone. I suppose it was an inspired attempt on my part to create a feeling of well being for all of us at that moment. As soon as the smells from the kitchen reached Kyle upstairs, we heard his activity accelerate, as though food was only then created and he had waited twelve years for his first bite.

Breakfast was more rushed than I would have liked and soon we were all filing out the door to begin another week of our lives. I grabbed my black attaché heavily laden with the subject matter for the afternoon's executive meeting and was out the door by 8:15 a.m.. Once in my car and having negotiated the residential streets of our well-groomed neighborhood, I became one link in an endless chain of vehicles drawn forward at a crippled pace by some unseen force. I found myself constantly looking for an opportunity to break free. But it was here, in this mundane traffic jam, that I was confined. I began to think about my day's activities. There would be the usual series of status reports on business development opportunities, government affairs issues and public affairs releases. I asked that each of my department directors provide such reports to me on Friday afternoons, so that I would have the information fresh in my mind on Monday morning should inquiries be made throughout the course of the week. I was also expecting to be interrupted throughout the morning with a series of calls on topics ranging from what I did over the weekend to the status of current alliances. I hoped and expected to be able to camouflage my uneasiness about the afternoon's executive meeting throughout my morning interactions.

Due to the heavier than usual morning traffic, I arrived at work ten minutes late. Messages had already begun to show on my voice-mail and my e-mail suggested that several of my managers were busy in the office over the weekend, as they had sent me messages describing emerging opportunities and issues for which they required my direction. And so the morning began.

Breaking with the morning routine I had anticipated in the car two hours earlier, I received an unexpected phone call from Catherine around 10:30 a.m..

"Hello, Ian, how's your morning been?" she inquired cautiously.

"Fine," I stated with a sigh, "How's yours been?"

Sensing I was curious as to why she had called me, Catherine replied, "Oh it's been OK, I guess. I just wanted to tell you that I'm thinking about you. I know that you've been preoccupied over the past few weeks with the problems at work and I know that you've got your executive meeting today. I just wanted you to know that I have every confidence in you, and that I love you."

"Thanks, Catherine, that means a lot to me," I added hesitantly. After a moment of silence, I filled the awkward vacancy with an acknowledgement of my own guilt, "I'm sorry for being so distracted lately. It's just that this investigation is tearing at me from every side. It'll be better once its resolved." I thanked her once again for the call and reminded her that if I'd be late for dinner, I'd let her know. Then we said our good-byes.

Hanging up the phone, I sat dazed for a moment trying to assess my emotions at that moment. There was a time when Catherine and I could speak for hours about almost anything. Now, I felt we struggled when we got beyond our initial greetings. Perhaps I was being overly sensitive? Maybe I was over-analyzing. I should simply have been pleased by the fact that she cared enough to phone and left it at that.

The rest of the morning passed quickly and at 12:30 p.m. I entered the executive boardroom where several colleagues had begun to gather around the buffet table. As per usual, a delicious four-course luncheon had been ordered for us, so I picked up a plate and began to scout out the offerings. Somehow, I was drawn into an inane conversation on sports franchises in Chicago but was saved from being exposed as a neophyte to professional sports by the arrival of Harold Stoner, Medicon's President and Chief Executive Officer.

The meeting began promptly at 1:00 p.m. and, following an excruciating twenty minutes of administrative issues, the agenda turned to a discussion of the investigation I was overseeing. The sound of my name pulled me back to the boardroom reality just as I was asked to comment on my findings and recommendations.

An endless hour of presentation, discussion and argument ensued and the ambient room temperature seemed to have risen twenty degrees. I was standing in the midst of my colleagues, all accomplished business people in their own right, but all consciously withholding a part of themselves from the discussion and from the company as a whole. What was the goal of every Vice President, if it wasn't to one day succeed in rising above their colleagues to be crowned President, so that their particular management style could be adopted throughout the firm? So it was in the beginning, so it shall always be. Still, in this process, I had to wonder: where was the rationality, the humanity? No one in the room wanted to rock the boat. No one would openly support the investigation and certainly no one would publicly denounce their colleagues' actions for fear that they too might fall some day and be renounced as a fool, or worse. And so it went, and so the fate of Medicon would be based on politics rather than on what was right.

Harold finally interrupted the debate and asked how I wished to proceed. I explained that two weeks had been an insufficient period of time to adequately address the issue and asked for a further month to determine the extent of the problem, to implicate those involved, to determine how Medicon was impacted, and to make recommendations on action. Several in the room seemed to perceive my positioning as bold, but Harold apparently wanted this dealt with properly and so gave me the time I needed, asking for a final report and presentation at the next executive meeting in one month. In addition, he insisted that everyone in the room be very quiet about the investigation. Furthermore, in front of all in attendance, he made it clear that he expected my loyalty to be to the executive throughout the investigation and made innuendo to the fact that advancement within the firm and indeed continued job security would be dependent upon such loyalty. The meeting concluded by 4:00 p.m. and I felt the wounds of my mental battering. As I made my way back to my office, I tried to console myself by remembering that no one promised me being an executive would be easy.

Once I got settled back at my desk, I called Paul and Karen into my office. Others amongst my staff were anxious to learn of the boardroom events for they knew that their own futures and mine hung in the balance. Before beginning to discuss my plan of action with the architects of the investigation, I spoke with my assistant Jackie for a moment.

Jackie Smythe, a 40-ish immigrant from Great Britain had always impressed me both for her efficiency and her dedication. Wife to a successful accountant and mother to an active seventeen-year-old son, she was best described as a professional woman whose time was torn between her career and her family, with little left for herself. She had been my administrative assistant for the past six years and throughout that time Catherine and I had invited the Smythe's to the house for dinner several times. Jackie had become a good friend who I had come to depend upon for advice, especially on issues where human behavior was in question, for she was highly intuitive. I trusted her completely.

Today, being well aware of the issues I faced and the stress they had created on me, she had kept my schedule clear and had chosen to wait until I volunteered information, rather than probing. I entered her office, adjacent to my own.

"Jackie, I'd like to bring the whole department together for a brief meeting. I'd rather have them hear how things went from me than from the rumor mill. Could you arrange to get a room and get everyone who's still here together in fifteen minutes?"

Obviously concerned, Jackie picked up her phone to begin corralling everyone together saying, "Of course, Ian. I'll do my best."

Understanding the torment she had endured waiting for weeks to see whether her job would survive the turmoil, I whispered to her, "Not to worry, Jackie. As long as I'm here, you're here. And I don't see them coming to get me yet."

She appreciated the gesture and it immediately seemed as if some of the weight had been lifted from her petite frame. I heard her busily calling the department managers, as I turned to reenter my office where Paul and Karen had arrived a moment before. I closed the door and sat down, sensing the anxiety in the room as I did so.

I began, "First, I want to commend both of you for the fine job you've done on this investigation. I realize this hasn't been easy for either of you or the others involved with you, both from a professional and a personal perspective. No one wants to be placed in a situation where they have to face the fact that the firm they work in is not the place they believed it to be. No one wants to face corruption in the workplace, or lies and deceit generated for the sole purpose of trying to conceal wrongdoing. And no one wants to believe that the senior executives who provide direction to the organization are guilty of abuses of privilege. No one wants to face these things, so I know how difficult it must be for you, two of Medicon's top contributors, to uncover these wrongdoings." I paused for a moment to interpret the looks on their faces. "With respect to this afternoon's executive meeting and what is to be done about your findings, I'll tell you that our work is not over yet. After deliberating for the past two weeks over your report and the supporting evidence, I felt I was insufficiently versed in enough of the details of the case to present it properly. As you both know, the implications of this report and my recommendations will be felt by many, including those accused and those doing the accusing. Therefore, I have to feel comfortable with my decisions."

"So does that mean these findings are going to be swept under the carpet?" Paul asked.

"Absolutely not," I assured him. "In fact, I asked Harold for a one-month period to study the issues further and then make recommendations back to the executive. Therefore, I'd like both of you to work with me closely over this period so we can achieve an outcome that is representative of our collective thinking."

"What about the rest of the team?" Karen asked, "Are they going to continue being involved?"

Pleased to hear Karen engaged in the defense of her team, I suggested, "I believe the majority of the work has been completed, so I think your three teammates can resume their routine responsibilities. We can always solicit their assistance if we require it. In the meantime, we need to develop criteria upon which to examine the evidence to determine whether those implicated have violated our customer trust, whether the firm has compromised its integrity with the public or its shareholders, and what impact these wrongdoings have had on our employees. Furthermore, we have to be aware of the implications of our recommendations on the customer, the shareholders, and the public at large."

Both Paul and Karen seemed relieved that their work was of value and that they would both have input with the final recommendations. In fact, I knew that I needed their analytical and perceptive abilities to review the investigation thoroughly.

"So," I suggested, "starting tomorrow, I'd like to meet with both of you from 10:00 a.m. to 2:00 p.m. each day, if you don't mind?" I also added that the entire investigation was to be kept highly confidential internally and externally and that any requests for information had to go through me. With that, I asked them to join me in a few minutes as I apprised the rest of my staff of the latest developments.

With the opening of my door, Jackie stood up, smiled at Paul and Karen, and upon their departure, joined me in my office.

"Of the thirty-seven staff, all but two are present and are congregating in Boardroom B on the fourth floor. Jim Nevins is ill today and Scott Pasko left early to pick up his daughter for a dentist's appointment. I'll arrange for them to meet with you tomorrow morning, if that's what you'd like."

Thanking Jackie again for her assistance, I grabbed some notes I had taken at the executive meeting and the two of us walked down the hall and two flights of stairs together before arriving in the room filled with my staff eagerly awaiting the report.

Whether my update to the group provided relief or provoked renewed anxiety as to the future of so many jobs at Medicon, I am uncertain. I suspect both feelings were experienced that afternoon by each staff member, including myself. In any event, due to my feelings of vulnerability over the few days that followed, I began to reflect upon what was important to me in my life. In doing so, I developed a renewed appreciation for my surroundings.

As an executive, I enjoyed the perks of the position which included such visible benefits as having a beautiful new Buick Park Avenue to drive. I remember getting the vehicle four months earlier in November of 1998. It was a blue so deep that at times it looked black, with tan leather inside and every conceivable option. It was a complete pleasure to drive. Then there was my office, a cliche in itself being situated in a corner of the sixth and top floor of Medicon's corporate center. Oak-paneled walls on two sides, lined with bookshelves, and then two walls of glass affording a view of a small park and forest immediately behind the building and, off in the distance, Chicago's impressive skyline. The building itself, finished extravagantly in chrome and glass and marble, was an icon of power and efficiency. There were unseen benefits, too, including club memberships, expense accounts, travel perks and superior treatment. I thought about how much I'd begun to take for granted each of these niceties and lamented over how much I'd miss them if Harold Stoner's threats were put into action. Pathetic as it was, I started to think that I'd been reduced to a materialistic bore, who sought validation for himself through the car he drove and the office he occupied. Not unlike the homeless person I had deafly ignored all too often on the streets of Chicago, my soul had been abandoned by an ego that found it easier to turn away.

And so, March marched on. Paul and Karen arrived dutifully each day with bulging file folders, prepared to continue with my briefing. The evidence was overwhelming as it was presented to me, along with an appropriate description as to how it was obtained. In the end, several senior management had been implicated. The facts described a situation wherein the Vice-President of Sales, Tod Slater, had made lavish personal expenses for his home, his friends and his family and charged them to the company through fraudulent expense claims made by many of his staff at his instruction. The ripple effect spread from the executive to two directors, through to six sales managers, and finally to twenty-one representatives, each of whom naively complied with their boss's requests. Noteworthy was the fact that Tod took the opportunity on numerous occasions to buy expensive gifts for Harold Stoner. Perhaps this was his way of buying support from the top.

More disturbing was the consequence that this manipulative action of deceit and betrayal had at the management level. It became apparent that harassment of representatives and sales managers occurred if they failed to comply with their superior's wishes, ultimately resulting in the departure of numerous talented individuals. Sexual misconduct was also noted by witnesses during sales meetings and training sessions, where managers felt they had the right to conduct themselves in an inappropriate manner in the presence of subordinates of the opposite sex. In general, an ethical anemia within the executive had created an environment where the truth throughout the organization was subverted. A lack of truth fostered mistrust, followed by compromised productivity and performance. When company expenses increased sharply and productivity fell, it was only a matter of time before corrective measures would be issued. When action was not taken, however, suspicions were raised. This was the situation that Paul and Karen had stumbled upon. Paul had been attempting to create a positive news release for Medicon throughout the Western states. A standard component of any press release was the sales figures and total company expenditures within each state. Collecting preliminary information was straightforward. However, he grew suspicious when the sales return on the investments made appeared unrealistic. Broadly speaking, the ratio of sales to expenses by state over a five-year period had been progressively deteriorating. It was Paul's tenacity and Karen's access to financial reports that led to the discovery and the need for further investigation.

Paul and Karen revealed the story to me over the next several days and our joint deliberation conclusively established the enormous scope of the problem. It was apparent that the outside world had not yet learned of any issue and likely never would. When the thought of disgruntled previous employees speaking out was considered, we reviewed the transcripts from interviews taken with these former staff. Even those who had been terminated harbored little ill will towards Medicon. This was likely because they had been coerced into believing that their dismissal was due to insubordination and therefore of their own doing or because they had put the issue behind them and had gone on to secure other employment. Consequently, we agreed that containment would be possible and was in the best interest of the company. After spending nearly two weeks grappling with the issues, the three of us began to lay out recommendations. I found Paul and Karen to be consistently more severe in disciplining the accused than I.

Perhaps I genuinely wanted to believe in the inherent goodness of people, or perhaps I had allowed my public humiliation at the board meeting to influence my decisions, but I felt it was necessary to personally revisit each of the recommendations that Karen, Paul and I had created. Specifically, I forced myself to reconsider those pertaining to each individual being accused in the investigation. Therefore, I dedicated the weekend of March 20th to the task and locked myself up in my home office to complete it alone. My mind was completely distracted. Losing my job in disgrace, being shunned by my executive colleagues, even thoughts of relinquishing my

new car played over and over again as I contemplated the recommendations that Karen, Paul and I had written only twen-
ty-four hours earlier. Karen and Paul had been dogmatic in
arguing that the discipline had to be simple and forceful. Fir-
ing Tod Slater and his two directors from the firm was
paramount. Following that, demoting the sales managers
involved and educating all representatives on appropriate
expense protocols was suggested. In addition, new policies on
harassment and abuse would be implemented indicating zero
tolerance. These were the major recommendations, which if
proposed to the executive, could easily cost Paul, Karen and
me our jobs and, depending how vindictive Mr. Stoner wished
to be, could exact a sizable toll on my department staff as well.
I had to come up with some solution to cover our butts. There
was no way I was going to put my career and security on the
line because of someone else's mismanagement of funds and
staff. Of this, I was sure, so I began to re-write the earlier recommendations that Karen and Paul had given to me.

As the hours passed, what began as modification, became
reconstruction. Words that previously spelled disaster for an employee's career had been erased. I resolved to
assume a posture of forgiveness where atonement for sins of
the past would guarantee an employee's future. I didn't
question why I felt comfortable to pass judgement on those
who had wronged so many others. In my dazed state, I
charged on, creating a new vernacular that would dress up
the recommendations Karen and Paul had established. My
suggestions included the following:

1. Human Resources would implement a sexual harass-
    ment prevention program and develop general
    harassment guidelines.

2. A position for an internal ombudsman would be created.

3. Tougher internal audits would be implemented.

4. Management implicated in this investigation would be formally warned.

5. No mention would be made of any executive involvement.

6. A new internal communications program would be developed to inform all staff of the new policies.

7. Special acknowledgement would be given to Paul Scott and Karen MacDonald for their efforts resulting in Medicon becoming a stronger and healthier organization.

Looking over these seven points, I felt as if they took action without being too aggressive. They let the executive know there had been an issue, but that it had been successfully controlled. They acknowledged those who had fallen and their comrades who helped them rise up to fight another day. Finally, and most importantly, these seven recommendations allowed me to remain loyal to the Medicon executive team.

I was pleased with myself. I carried this satisfying feeling with me to work the following Monday, along with the knowledge that within a few short weeks I would have an opportunity to share this news with the executive. Until then, I resigned myself to keeping the progress that had been made quiet. I did need to meet with Paul and Karen, however, to explain the changes I had made. I also wanted to congratulate them for their work over the previous six months or so and reward them with some time off or something, though I hadn't yet given much thought to how I would acknowledge their hard work. As I waited for their now routine arrival at my office at 10:00 a.m., I remember appreciating my morning coffee a bit more than usual that day. "Yes, I am doing the right thing," I told myself as I glanced out the window towards the downtown skyline. "This is best for everyone."

Paul and Karen shared a similar stunned expression as they read my report. Incredulously, they asked if I was serious and what had caused me to shift my opinion so significantly. Surprised by their candor, I began to piece together an argument. I explained that they had to appreciate that, as the Vice-President responsible for the entire department, I had to look at the big picture both for the future of the firm and the future of the department. The human toll this issue had already exacted had to be weighed along with the fact that no external damage had yet been caused, the latter of which had been prevented primarily because of their hard work and diplomacy. I made it clear that I recognized that the two of them had preserved the company's reputation in the market, had prevented a probable slide in stock price, and had undoubtedly saved dozens of jobs that otherwise would have been sacrificed due to shareholder dissatisfaction. Despite the level of enthusiasm in my voice and my conviction about my weekend's deliberations, Karen and Paul were obviously upset. I hated to leave them high and dry, but with a lunch engagement that day, I had to draw our meeting to a close, so I asked if they would join me for coffee later that afternoon at the café Paul and I had visited once before. They apathetically agreed to meet me at 3:00 p.m., and then left my office in silence. Despite their sullenness, I felt like a father having successfully consoled his jilted daughter over a boyfriend that just never measured up to dad's expectations. While moved by her sadness, I was secretly jubilant that the suitor would be taking up residence elsewhere.

With renewed confidence following an extraordinarily productive lunch, I arrived ten minutes early at the cafe and was able to find a comfortable suite of plush chairs surrounding a unique triangular-shaped table. A few other patrons were in the cafe that afternoon as well and everyone seemed relaxed by the soulful rhythms of a familiar jazz recording. A middle-aged couple in one corner sipped their drinks slowly and, then, only to punctuate shared phrases of obvious affection. A young woman read a dog-eared novel silently at a small table in the center of the floor, oblivious to the rest of the world. An athletic, tall, black man, probably in his sixties, who had arrived a moment before me, was served his coffee by the counter staff and carried himself confidently to a large armchair behind my own. And two elderly women, apparently resting from a day of shopping and hair treatments, occupied a table across the room. Having completed my visual survey, Karen and Paul arrived.

After ordering our drinks, we immediately revisited our morning discussion and I asked them what their concerns were. Their feedback, although much the same as that offered earlier in the day, seemed to be mellowed by the comfort of our surroundings and the gentle rhythms of the music. Despite their dissent, I felt confident that their needs could be met. They shared with me their own feelings towards the accused parties and the toll the damage had taken on the Medicon culture. Staff who once praised the firm for its humanity, were now feeling a moral void. Others were deprived of hope by what they felt had been indifference from the executive. Paul and Karen themselves shared with me the toll this exercise had exacted on them personally and how they felt morally challenged each day. They expressed uncertainty about their future in working for a firm that would condone such reprehensible behavior. I assured them that decisive action would be taken but that we also needed to move on for the sake of the organization. Despite my upbeat demeanor and positive tone, I could tell they were disappointed with me. After ninety minutes of exchange, Karen and Paul left the cafe, presumably to seek consolation elsewhere. Feeling gradually more pensive and deflated, I ordered another latté and tried to allow my confused mind to find refuge and my wounded soul to find solace in this place that was increasingly becoming a sanctuary from the rest of my life.

4

Letting Life
Pre-empt Living

I found it surprisingly easy to get distracted in this place. With the warm tones of the music and furnishings to cushion the heaviest of thoughts, the atmosphere was inviting and somehow vaguely familiar to me. I groped through my memory trying to recall where I had been before that evoked such memories. Had it been on my trips abroad to Paris or Vienna or Venice? Had I heard these sounds in a jazz club downtown here in Chicago or when I last visited New Orleans? I couldn't quite place this feeling, but then I didn't really need to. All that was important to me now was the wonderfully distracting peace.

As I sat comfortably, soaking up my surroundings, I closed my eyes every so often and allowed the music to take me away. Following one of these brief departures, I opened my eyes to find a large figure looking down at me. Startled, I looked up and found the face of the same gentleman who had been sitting directly behind me for the past two hours peering down at me through playful eyes. He asked if I would mind some company and I stammered out the first thought in my head, "Certainly, please join me."

"Karl's my name, Karl Lawrence," he volunteered as he pulled up the large chair beside my own.

Feeling a bit uneasy, I replied, "I'm Ian Archer. It's a pleasure to meet you, Karl." Now, despite the fact that I'd pursued a career where meeting new people was second nature, a part of me was quite reserved. There were times when I appreciated and valued my privacy, especially within the general public. In fact, I often cautioned myself: What do I know about this person? What do they do? What are their motivations? Engaging in a conversation with a complete stranger might compromise my privacy or jeopardize my security, I told myself. It's amazing how paranoid I'd become over the years. I wasn't always like this, nor was this the way I wanted to be now. Too many others these days were like this. So many, in fact, it appeared as if distrust had become a right of passage for twenty-first-century citizens living in urban centers. It didn't use to be this way. It shouldn't have to be this way. But I resigned myself sadly to the apparent truth that it was this way, like it or not.

Karl explained he was a recently retired college professor. "Biology," he added, "For thirty years I taught general biology classes, taxonomy, zoology, and ethology."

"What exactly is that?" I asked.

"Ethology's the study of animal behavior, zoology's the study of animals, and taxonomy's the classification of living organisms," he explained.

I informed Karl that I had been a student of biology and that I had studied taxonomy and zoology but was not familiar with the term "ethology".

"It's my greatest passion," Karl answered. "To understand why living creatures do what they do has always fascinated me. Since retiring, I've found myself analyzing human behavior whenever I have the opportunity. That's one of the reasons I enjoy coming here. There's always something different to see. Humans exhibit the most complex of behaviors, often paradoxical, and many times not exhibited by any other species."

With a wry smile, I suggested, "That's likely a good thing."

"There's an aspect of truth in what you say," Karl added. "In the four months I've been visiting this place, I've witnessed that, in general, people congregate here not only for the great coffee but to escape from the world for a time and find some peace in their lives. To be soothed and comforted, to seek refuge from life's pain, this is why such places exist. We humans have a great need for these things in our lives, but seldom admit that fact to ourselves and even more infrequently do anything about it. Instead, we stumble along approaching life as a young apprentice approaches his trade: eager, well-intentioned, and prepared for failure."

His words were strung together rhythmically and I found myself captivated by the cadence of his voice. I wanted to learn more from this man who had obviously much to teach. But almost as startling as his arrival had been, was his sudden departure.

"I must be going, now," he said. "But before I leave, let me ask you, Ian Archer. What is your pain?"

I was caught unprepared for the question and therefore my parting glance at Karl was accompanied with stunned silence. I sat for another twenty minutes thinking about this man and his question. Wasn't it presumptuous of him to ask something so personal of a stranger? Maybe he was unstable? Or perhaps he'd overheard my conversation with Karen and Paul and was attempting to get me to think about my decisions further? I was unsure of myself now. Karl appeared by all accounts to be an educated man and I found his insights appealing, at least until they were directed at me. I was sure I was being overly sensitive to his question. I should have just forgotten about it. But it stayed with me, like a song that gets stuck in your head in the morning and plays in your mind all day until you end up singing it yourself. Such was the case with Karl's question. I started to ask myself, "What is my pain?" So many thoughts came to mind. Was it my job? Perhaps it was having to make decisions that didn't meet everyone's needs? Maybe it was simply the issue that I was facing at that moment in time? It could've been the pain I shared with Karen and Paul as a result of the moral bankruptcy that had plagued Medicon for some time. Then again, my pain could have been even more fundamental than this. It could have been the result of my own deteriorating feelings of self-fulfillment or self-worth. I didn't know, and soon I grew tired of second guessing myself so I pulled myself out of the comfy embrace of the chair I'd been sitting in for the past few hours, paid the cashier and stepped outside to begin my journey home.

It was 6:00 p.m. when I got home. Catherine had warned me that she might be late and she was. Kyle was oblivious to this fact as he'd simply thrown his knapsack on the front steps and had engaged his friends in their routine game of after-school street hockey. A child-care arrangement we'd made with a neighbor allowed us to always be sure of Kyle's safety, but most days he simply tossed his books on the step and played with his friends until Catherine or I arrived home. Although the days were getting noticeably longer, the street was beginning to darken when I pulled into the driveway. I looked through my car window and smiled at the scene before me. I was transported back through time to the days of my youth when I used to play hockey in the streets of Dorval with my friends. I remember teaching my brother Shawn how to hold the stick and eventually how to play the game. After moving to New York, sometimes Dad would tear himself from his latest project to get in on the action, especially when we found ourselves to be a man short. I could picture him back then, thirty years younger, with his plaid flannel shirt, jeans and a well-worn carpenter's apron out there chasing after the hockey ball. Those were good times I told myself, as I snapped my thoughts back to the present. Simpler times.

Getting out of my comfortable car, I waved to Kyle and told him it was time to call it a night. Luckily for us, Kyle had always been respectful of Catherine and myself and so was quick to say good night to his friends. He beat a path to the front steps, where he retrieved his backpack and joined me at the opened door.

"How was your day, Dad?" he inquired with his usual enthusiasm.

"I had an interesting day today, Kyle," I responded vaguely. "Yeah, interesting is probably the best way to describe it."

"That's great, Dad. Oh, guess what? The baseball try-outs were posted today; they start in three weeks time. I can hardly wait. And yesterday at hockey practice the coach gave us the playoff schedule. Games start in just over a week. I think Mom's got the sheet with the times on it."

"It sounds as if you're going to be busy over the next couple of weeks," I said. By that time, we had settled into the kitchen where I began to look through the refrigerator for dinner ideas. Kyle had found a banana and proceeded to inhale it while remarking in half-garbled tones about the events of his day.

After dinner, I sent Kyle upstairs to do his homework, while I poured myself a glass of Merlot and settled into my study. I was soon busy recounting my "interesting" day in my mind. Paul and Karen were terribly disappointed with me, my luncheon meeting with a new business partner went extraordinarily well, and a gentleman I'd never met before asked what pained me. And then there was my son, bless his soul, whom I found to be growing by leaps and bounds in front of my eyes. Sipping my wine, I considered each of these things in isolation. I could feel my passion for work being extinguished by all the malicious politics of the office. I'd lost my spark. I was worn out. My mental gymnastics continued without resolution until I heard the garage door opening. Catherine was home. Glancing at the brass clock on my desk, I noticed it was a quarter to nine.

I greeted her at the door with a hug and a kiss and inquired about her day.

"Too long," was her annoyed reply.

"Did you manage to grab something to eat?" I asked.

"Yeah, we ordered some Chinese food. But I could really go for a glass of wine right now. Is there any left?"

I began to wonder whether after smelling the wine on my breath she was upset with me. "You go ahead and take your shower and relax and I'll bring you up a glass," I offered. As Catherine hung up her coat and climbed the stairs to our bedroom, I felt uneasy. Ours was a polite and caring relationship, but it was getting increasingly obvious to me that something was missing between us.

Never before in our marriage had I spent so much time distractedly thinking about my family, my employment, and my past as I had over the previous two weeks. I'm sure Catherine sensed my distraction as well, for it was more than simply those few weeks that we barely spoke with one another. A distance had been emerging between us for several years. In fact, we'd both suggested at different times over the past two years the idea of visiting a family therapist, but coordinating our schedules seemed impossible. There were the usual commitments to our respective employers, there was the increasingly harried sports schedule for Kyle, my involvement with the local community association, and with various industry groups. Then there were Catherine's fitness classes, her pottery lessons, and a symphony of personal wellness lectures and symposia she attended. In fact, due to the pace of our lives, we'd decided not to have a second child. I remember so clearly struggling with that decision. Although Catherine was an only child and didn't object to adhering to the same model for our family, that wasn't the case with me. I was raised very close to Marie and Shawn and numerous cousins and always enjoyed a large and extended family and community. I had

wanted Kyle to experience that, but instead had compromised my dream by rationalizing that we couldn't be the
type of parents we wished to be with an infant, given all our
other commitments. That was five years ago. Then there
was my mother's illness, followed by her death. And time
had a habit of just marching forward with reckless regard
for the intentions of the well-meaning people left in its
wake. And we fell hapless victims to a life that seemed to be
controlled more by society than ourselves, where living out
our uncomplicated dreams was impossible. It was never a
case that we didn't take our marriage seriously, though. We
told ourselves that we could self-counsel. We attended several workshops designed to bring couples closer together
and it all helped alleviate the symptoms, but in hindsight we
never addressed the cause of our growing discontent. The
problem all along had not been apparent to either of us. We
loved one another, shared mutual respect, had a wonderful
son, great jobs, we traveled, and had no material desires
that hadn't been or couldn't be met. I told myself that perhaps it was just the pace of life in general for both of us. In
fact, when we had vacationed together, we always seemed
to find ourselves again. That's probably what it was. I was
sure that all couples experienced the same thing. Life was so
hectic. Everyone acknowledged that. Catherine and I just
needed to get away for a little while.

I put Catherine's glass of wine down on the bedside
table and announced to her through the slightly ajar bath-
room door that it and I were awaiting her presence. At that
moment she shut off the water, grabbed a towel and stepped
out onto the bathmat. Perched on our bed, I watched as she
dried herself. At thirty-five, she was as beautiful as the first
day I had met her. Her hair, cropped to shoulder length, was

pure chestnut in color. Her body was well-toned and her olive skin tight. I enjoyed the curves of her form now as much as I ever had. Slipping a shimmering satin nightgown over her body, she joined me in our bedroom, raised her glass, and toasted to our good health. In response, I offered a toast to her, my beautiful wife. After kissing Kyle good night, we retreated to our room and spent the next hour that evening talking about our respective employment challenges. She explained the problems that had emerged with a client of hers who continued to shift his expectations, while I explained my discussion with Karen and Paul. I also mentioned that I might be travelling and that we needed to take a vacation soon, just the two of us. Catherine felt that would be a wonderful idea and proposed Hawaii. We agreed to check our calendars the following day. Fatigued and comforted by the wine and the words we drifted off to sleep in each other's arms.

Tuesday morning I decided it would be best for all concerned to engage Karen and Paul in new assignments. Paul had broad public relations responsibilities including a new Medicon promotional campaign designed to raise public awareness of the firm, its products, and the research being performed. It was argued that such advertising would enhance shareholder interest and stock value. Therefore, at our daily 10:00 a.m. meeting, I asked Paul to revisit the program and establish some timelines for regional launching of the media spots. I deployed Karen in the business development department doing what she did best, analyzing the financial viability of new business opportunities. Although they both committed themselves to doing their best, I could tell that new work assignments would not serve as prosthetics for their amputated spirits. I would have to manage them carefully over the next few months, or they would be lost to Medicon.

Two more days of routine work and I was beginning to feel things around the office returning to normal. There were the usual meetings to attend, project status reports to review, a division to run and new business opportunities to assess. It was with respect to the latter that I received a call on the morning of Thursday, March 18th from Medicon's new alliance partner, which resulted in me clearing my calendar and calling my travel agent. I had been invited to examine several key aspects of our partner's business operations in London, Hamburg, Lisbon and Geneva, followed by stops in Santiago, Buenos Aires, Singapore and Tokyo before returning home. I would be travelling for ten days, visiting manufacturing facilities, logistics centers, as well as several clients, and I had to leave in two days.

I picked up my phone, "Jackie, could you please join me in my office for a few minutes?"

"Of course," she replied apprehensively.

Before entering, Jackie gently knocked on my half-opened door. "Come in and have a seat," I offered. In hindsight I should have been more sensitive to the fact that, for months, my assistant and the rest of my staff for that matter had been very nervous about the rumored company downsizing and restructuring. When I called her into my office that Thursday morning, Jackie was particularly uneasy and I could see a tear forming in the corner of her eye. I'm sure, now, she felt she was about to be dismissed from Medicon.

Trying to avoid any embarrassment, I quickly reassured her, "Jackie, I have only good news to tell you." Her relief was tangible.

"Oh, what's that Ian?"

"Well, I'm going to be out of your hair for ten days. So you'll have to keep this well-oiled machine of a division humming until I get back, OK?" I said only half-jokingly, knowing that she could do the job expertly. "I was hoping that you could book my travel arrangements for me."

Accustomed to my likes and dislikes while travelling, she replied with a smile on her face, "Where are you off to, and for how long in each destination?"

After providing all the particulars, she rose to leave. "Should I send flowers to Catherine this afternoon?"

"Please do, and the usual chocolate truffles as well," I urged.

"Of course, Ian, and I'll have two copies of your itinerary for your personal use on your desk this afternoon and a third copy for circulation as well," Jackie offered.

Now, for most, the prospect of international travel may hold appeal. But for those who are required to travel as a part of their job, it can become terribly burdensome, especially if it involves juggling schedules within the home. This was definitely the case with us. We were busy at the best of times, but when one of us was not available to make dinner or to shuttle Kyle around or to be there for him, life became way too stressful. When I travelled, I made a point of recognizing the added burden to Catherine through small gifts such as flowers and chocolates. Tacky maybe, but nonetheless sincere. I've been on the other side of the fence myself, when Catherine is called out of town on assignments and so I know the disruption is real. I just like to let her know I appreciate the extra effort she has to make to keep things together while I am gone.

Despite my dislike of so many flights, a different bed every night, airplane food and harried work schedules while travelling, I have to admit that I actually selfishly enjoy getting away from my life for a while. Although I never told anyone this, I found that travelling on business afforded me a welcome departure from the usual Monday to Friday routine. I got to deal with different people than those within the office, seek resolutions to different issues, enjoy different scenery, perhaps different food, different cultures and different music. I didn't need to be preoccupied with the volume of traffic, or with getting dinner started, or with transporting Kyle to his next commitment. Nor did I have to be concerned at the end of the day with Catherine's moods. While travelling, I could focus on my needs for a change. I felt irresponsible and unsympathetic thinking these selfish thoughts, but I indulged myself nonetheless.

With this momentary lapse of self-indulgence behind me, my thoughts turned more seriously to Catherine and I realized I had to take ownership for much of the bad temper that soured our relationship. Too frequently I felt isolated at work and at home, overcome with moments of loneliness and anxiety. I asked myself whether my work situation had crept its way into my personal life like some insidious disease overtaking my body, or if my dissatisfaction in my relationship with Catherine over the past several years had spread to my work life? I tried to remember back through the years to determine what had happened first.

Nine years ago when we made the move to Chicago, both Catherine and I deeply felt the changes in our lives. After all, Chicago was no Palo Alto. Nonetheless, we were both excited at the possibilities that lay ahead for us as a family. After Catherine returned to work, her passion to prove herself to the partners within her consulting practice translat-

ed into many long days. The daily commute to and from the city just added to the stress and subtracted from her time with the family. Although her extra effort was noticed and she became a valuable asset to her employer, the accolades and rewards simply fueled her desire to achieve even more. It was as if the Pavlovian reflex had become engrained in her psyche. She behaved as though she had something to prove to herself and to those within her world. Admittedly, I did nothing but support her on her quest, for I seldom remarked on her long hours or her absence from Kyle and me. I felt that as a supportive husband I must encourage and praise her for her many career accomplishments.

My own schedule did little to suggest anything other than the fact I condoned this pace of life. I, too, was busy in my own world trying to impress and to cross that most difficult of barriers into the ranks of the senior executives of the firm. For a time I believed that I need only do my best at my job, be an effective leader, be patient, and the rest would come. In fact, I remain certain to this day that this would have been the case had Scott Ashbury, the former president of Medicon, not retired.

Scott had brought me into the Medicon family. During my interviews, I had felt an inexplicable bond with him. I related to the type of organization he wished to create, both in terms of growth and financial performance, but also in terms of human empowerment. I trusted him and he reciprocated. He was my mentor, my coach in the corporate world. He was highly principled in all aspects of his life and made employment at Medicon a wonderful experience for everyone. But three years after my arrival his health deteriorated and at the age of sixty he departed, allowing Harold Stoner to ascend to the top post. And with Stoner's control over the firm, there came an entirely different perspective on business. I knew that advancement would be dependent upon playing the corporate game under a new set of rules and so I dedicated myself to learning how to play. That was the case until about five years ago when my family life became simply a collection of commitments and obligations. Two weekly diaries crossed in the night, devoid of any meaning. Then Mom was diagnosed with breast cancer and life for us hit its lowest mark. The year and a half that followed was riddled with numerous visits to the old homestead, helping out Dad whenever I could, going to the hospitals, arguing with doctors, and making Mom as comfortable as possible. After her passing, I felt that the sanctuary she had created for me had slipped away with her.

Life in Chicago seemed to change after that. Both Catherine and I felt our vulnerabilities and our mortality, but we reacted differently. Catherine pulled back from her work somewhat and began to invest more time in herself. She attended seminars on wellness and ancient healing practices, I think prompted by research she had done on Mom's illness. To relax, she began to take pottery classes. In contrast, I immersed myself in my work and blindly stumbled into a cavernous pit of vacant souls. Too insecure to

*grope for answers and too proud to retreat, I
remained static in a world that was changing all
around me. Ironically, it was during this period of
disconnect that I was offered the Corporate Development post. At the time of the announcement I
recall Stoner suggesting to me that he had recognized my demeanor would synchronize well with
the rest of the executive team. In hindsight, I should
have been leary of such a proclamation. After all,
I'd spent the previous year walking around the
office like a dispassionate zombie. But I slept right
through this wake-up call. And Catherine was too
caught up with her own stuff to recognize what had
happened in me. Had this been the catalyst of my
current state of unhappiness? I'm sure it was a part
of the story, but there had to be more to it than that.*

The sudden sound of a flock of geese flying by overhead
interrupted my train of thought and encouraged me to look
out the window. I marveled at their aerodynamic formation,
a perfect V, but for one lone goose who was obviously
injured and had fallen back a considerable distance. Its cries
struck a chord with me, and I found myself cheering for the
lame bird in the hopes that my silent support would provide
the strength it needed to catch up to the flock. I had always
loved to watch geese, though with some bittersweetness, for
their appearance usually meant that change in the weather,
in the seasons, in the cycle of life itself—was inevitably
afoot and I wasn't necessarily sure I was ready for it. Furthermore, although I admired the grace and speed with
which they flew, I was also envious of their capacity to fly.
If only I could up and fly away, leaving all my troubles
behind. Given the travel preparations I'd made earlier in the

day, the irony of this thought suddenly struck me: In many respects, I would be doing just that in less than 48 hours.

I spent the rest of my day addressing routine issues. My benign agenda gave me license to revisit my history in this building several more times before departing that day.

By 4:00 p.m. the afternoon was gone for all intents and purposes, so I packed my briefcase with a few articles on emerging medical technologies, tossed in the two copies of my travel itinerary, wished Jackie a pleasant evening, and left for the day. As I approached my Buick at the front of the building, I admired the way the afternoon sun teased out the deep blue of the paint. Glancing at my Rolex, another company perk given to all executives at the last Christmas party, I realized I had no reason to be home so early. I decided to treat myself to a cappuccino.

The café was becoming a welcome oasis to me, so it wasn't surprising that I felt in better spirits as I pulled my car in front of the collection of shops that shared the same building. I wondered to myself whether I would see Karl Lawrence again or whether he was simply a creation of my imagination. As I grabbed the handle to the door, I reflected over our previous encounter and wondered whether the question posed—"What is your pain?"—was actually conjured from within my own mind, or from one who would be more demanding in seeking an answer. I entered the shop to find only one other patron and it wasn't the man I'd seen before. With mixed feelings over not having had an opportunity to further engage the professor, I ordered my beverage and sank into one of the heavenly chairs. I positioned my back to the far wall, so I could enjoy the afternoon sun shining in through the windows across the room while also watching for familiar faces that might enter this peaceful place.

As I spooned the cinnamon-topped froth of my cappuccino and allowed the sun to brush softly across my face, I became contemplative. "What is my pain?" I asked myself softly. The words reverberated in my mind like an echo. I even unconsciously began to write the question over and over again on the paper napkin in front of me. As though my life were a record with a subtle yet damaging scratch across its surface, the day's ruminations skipped over and over again. Why, after all those years, I had decided to finally address my problems that afternoon, I don't know. Maybe it was because so many aspects of my life seemed to be tugging at me at that time. As patrons entered and left and the mug in front of me revealed nothing but the residue of another hour of quiet soul-searching, I resigned myself to the knowledge that the answers would not be found that day.

I believe now that my reluctance in leaving the café that Thursday evening was because I felt as if Life was my master and I was nothing more than its puppet, being pulled this way and that by the strings of fear, obligation and guilt.

I eventually did pull myself away and arrived home that evening a few minutes before 6:00 p.m.. Catherine was already home and by the smells that were permeating the house I could tell she was preparing a wonderful Thai beef dish that she had perfected many years before. The flowers I had sent were positioned on the table in the front foyer. I had really outdone myself this time! The arrangement was large and contained a wide array of tropical species that were foreign to me. By virtue of its prominent placement in the house, I presumed that Catherine was pleased.

"Hello," I called out as I hung up my overcoat.

"Hi, honey, I'm in here," she replied cheerfully.

I entered the kitchen to find my wife in shorts and a T-shirt singing and swinging to the music on the radio. Dinner was close to being ready.

"Well, you look like you're having a good time in here," I said with a chuckle. "What's up?"

"Kyle phoned me at the office this afternoon to ask if he could go to a friend's for dinner after hockey practice. He's gonna get a ride home around nine, so I thought it would be a perfect time to have something spicy with you," she winked. "Oh, and thank you for the flowers, they're wonderful, sweetheart," she added as she pecked me on the cheek.

"You're welcome, love," I said kissing her perfumed neck. "Now, let me go and get cleaned up and then maybe after dinner we could talk about a little vacation."

"You've got ten minutes before it hits the plate," she called out as I darted upstairs feeling carefree for a change. After a quick shower, I jumped into my jeans and a T-shirt and, convinced that I had washed away the issues that had pre-occupied me that day, I joined my effervescent wife for dinner. The deliciously spicy food was accompanied by a few mandatory ice-cold Corona. Not surprisingly, after eating, we were inspired to change the destination of our vacation to Cancun. Selecting a mutually agreeable departure time, however, was not as straightforward. After discussing our schedules for half an hour, we both conceded to check with our respective offices the following day for the first available opportunity. The conversation proved to be sobering to us both, so after saying goodnight to Kyle at 9:30 p.m., we both retired as well, with no intentions other than sleep.

Friday was a busy day preparing for my impending trip and assuring that my responsibilities would be covered in my absence. In fact, I had little time to even think about a vacation let alone plan for one. No matter how I looked at my upcoming itinerary over the months that lay ahead, taking a vacation any time soon was simply irresponsible. That evening, Catherine's news was no more positive than my own. It seemed that we had expected as much of the other, so little more was said on the subject. I packed my bags for the next day's departure and went to bed early, as I knew that my trip would be exhausting.

The following morning, Saturday, the 20th of March, after kissing Catherine and Kyle good-bye, I took a cab to O'Hare airport with a head jammed full of thoughts. That's the only way I can describe the impact that the previous month's events had had on me. I was mentally cluttered and I desperately hoped that over the next ten days I'd begin to find some reprieve from it all.

5

A Man in Crisis

Finding myself amidst thousands of people in one of the world's largest and busiest airports on a Saturday morning was not my idea of a good time. Sixty-five million people scurry around O'Hare each year. Regrettably, it appeared that most of them decided that that particular Saturday was their day for travel. There were people lined up within mazes of rope barriers extending for thousands of feet just waiting for their turn at the front of the line, only to then be directed to the security clearance queue which was just as long. Then there were the cries of children who were bored and the sharp retorts of tired parents who were constantly fearful of losing their charges. All of this I could see and feel while waiting in the relatively peaceful executive check-in line. I was empathetic for those parents for I'd been in the same situation half a dozen times before. I remember on one occasion when Kyle was about seven, he slipped away from Catherine and me at the airport in Miami. I found him five minutes later engaged in a conversation with two girls of about the same age. Although obviously relieved to have recovered him unscathed, the thoughts of misfortune that fill a parent's head at times like that are scarier than any horror flick Hollywood could offer.

Perhaps the empathy I felt reveals a subtle bond amongst humans, a personal connection that transcends routine societal behavior, enabling a parent to feel protective of all children, not just their own. It's as if the act of rearing children confers on parents some sort of membership in a greater fraternity wherein certain privileges of trust and caring are shared. I shivered in recognition of this enormous responsibility as my check-in line moved forward again with a familiar cadence.

Passing through international security clearance was again a painfully slow process. Over my many years of travel, however, I had learned to rationalize the pace, knowing that my safety would be assured as a result. Within an hour and a half of my arrival at the airport, I finally made my way into the secure vestibule for international departures and located my gate. I recall having noticed the diversity of nationalities that were boarding my flight to Heathrow that morning, and from this fascination, I began to wonder what type of project an enterprising student like Kyle could do by interviewing the people at an airport such as this? Between these rather trivial thoughts and my morning newspaper, I occupied my time.

Boarding my flight, I felt a wave of apprehension overcome me as I thought about the next two weeks. That I'd be exhausted at the end of this trip was obvious, but having to return to face Medicon's executive aroused an unsavory dread in me. Regardless, I settled into my comfortable seat and surrendered to the hospitality of premiere-class travel.

The dinner wine and cognac allowed me to sleep through most of the flight, so I found the first leg of my journey rather uneventful. Arriving in Heathrow at 11:00 p.m. local time, I was amazed to find a driver awaiting me, courtesy of Biocodon, Medicon's new strategic alliance partner. Although based in Oxford largely due to the brain trust the company had established there, Biocodon had been developing into a global biotechnology firm with research operations throughout Europe, Canada, and Japan, and with manufacturing sites in Argentina and Chile. Since I was ultimately responsible for ensuring the credibility of all of our alliance partners, I always made a point of conducting a thorough site analysis of all operations prior to committing Medicon. This was the rationale for my travels over the next ten days.

Biocodon had recently entered the field of cancer diagnostics and therapeutics as a result of a series of promising findings out of Oxford University's Institute for Molecular Medicine. These findings were subsequently embellished upon by data in Lisbon and Geneva. I found myself excited at the prospect of being at the cusp of a new wave in cancer research, while also appreciating the income potential that a lucrative license with Biocodon could bring my own firm. Perhaps this relationship with Biocodon was just what I needed to reset my spiritual equilibrium.

As fate would have it, my host, Nathan Currie, was to be in London on the evening of my arrival and had therefore suggested I stay overnight in the city to allow us the opportunity to travel to Oxford together in the morning. To my surprise, though, my late arrival at the hotel was met with greetings from the man himself.

As I walked through the impressive front door, the gray-haired man of fifty offered an enthusiastic outstretched hand and declared, "Ian Archer, it's so good to see you again."

"Dr. Currie, it's a pleasure," I said, surprised that he was still up at this hour.

"It is indeed. What's it been, four months since our meeting in Chicago?"

Correcting him, I said, "Perhaps a little longer."

"No matter, it's been too long, and there's much to talk about, but first I'm sure you are exhausted and would like to settle into your room. How would it be if I met you for brunch here at the restaurant tomorrow around 11:00 a.m.?"

"Eleven sounds wonderful," I said shaking his hand goodnight.

With that, he smiled and left for his room. I stood in the two-hundred year-old hotel lobby for a moment somewhat amazed by what I'd just experienced. The airport greeting, a car into the city, a personal welcome from a friendly face, and an invitation for brunch in the morning were each very much appreciated. It had been some time since I felt so relaxed as an executive and so respected as a human being. In my travels over the years, I'd become aware of various cultural biases towards business and in fact had experienced first-hand numerous practices I found to be unusual in many areas of the world. Despite all of our differences, though, the importance of respect seemed to be a common thread uniting all cultures. So, why had I suddenly been taken aback by simple courteous behavior? Wouldn't I do the same for my guests? My head was suddenly feeling tired of all the analysis so I let my thoughts dissipate as I checked in and navigated the corridors of the hotel to my room. Despite my misgivings that night for having slept on the plane earlier, I eventually found sedation in the words of a scientific report I was reviewing and enjoyed seven hours of sound sleep.

I awoke at 8:00 a.m., annoyed by the commotion of pigeons, buses, and other sounds indigenous to London's streets on a Sunday morning. After a workout in what obviously had been a recently constructed fitness center, I showered, dressed and began to absorb the words in The Sunday Times. Soon, I was accompanied by Nathan and engrossed in a wonderful discussion of his past and Biocodon's future.

As the story was relayed to me that morning, Nathan Currie had been born in Yorkshire, the youngest of eight children. His father was a bookkeeper for a textile firm and instilled strong moral values in all of his children. He was nearly fifty by the time Nathan was born, so all of Nathan's memories were of a man who, despite valiant attempts to disguise the fact, had already lived his best years. George Currie was often tired, but always found time for his family. Nathan's mother, not unlike my own, worked endlessly within the home raising a large family and preserving harmony and order. With little money to spare, family entertainment was for the most part comprised of story telling, singing, and sporting activities in which they all engaged together. Nathan spoke of the pride his parent's felt when he won scholarships to university, for he was the first Currie to go on to higher education. It was obvious to me that these were profoundly moving recollections for Nathan, for with many of the memories recounted, water would form in the corners of his eyes and each time the stoic scientist would fight back the tears. He praised his parents for their values and for the way he and his siblings were made to feel so special. He told me of his father's pride at seeing his youngest child graduate from university and his own anguish when George passed away from lung cancer one year later. As if baptized in resolve, Nathan spoke of his determination after that point to dedicate his life to finding cures to the illnesses of man. That journey took the young science student to graduate school at Berkeley in California, followed by a return to England to attend Oxford University in pursuit of a doctorate in molecular genetics. Listening to the man's compelling story, I believed myself to be in the company of one much wiser and more experienced despite the rather modest seven year age gap between us. I took from this a positive feeling that, in time, I too might be in a position to impart wisdom.

Nathan continued on at my insistence. He spoke as passionately about Biocodon and the promise of new research as he did about his family. Evident in our discussions over the past eleven months was a palpable soulfulness that was apparent in everything the man loved. It could be heard in his phrases, the careful inflections in his voice, the spirited expressions on his face, and the animated arm movements that accompanied each exclamation. This was a man who lived honestly, whose promise was the sinew of his being, who would rather fail in life than compromise his principles. This man could be trusted. Though I'd known him for only a brief time, the moments we had shared made me feel so at ease, so comfortable. I felt as if Nathan could be someone I would want to call a friend. I'm sure it was his many exceptional traits that led me to Biocodon in the first place and they certainly contributed to my agreement to pursue the strategic alliance on behalf of Medicon.

Following our brunch I checked out of the hotel, for Nathan and I would be off to Geneva that evening. A driver and car were awaiting us as we left, and within minutes we were on our way to Oxford. Nathan explained that having a car and driver was not only a nice and luxurious way to descend upon the "City of Dreaming Spires," but was also an efficient way to spend a couple hours talking business without the distraction of driving or navigating ourselves. In fact, chauffeured transportation was so contrary to the simple life that Nathan Currie had established for himself that he felt compelled to explain it to me.

With an understanding smile on my face, I stated, "Nathan, there's no need to feel embarrassed. I understand this isn't your usual form of transportation. Be that as it may, I'll tell you that I feel flattered you would have taken the time to think about our itinerary in such detail. Meeting me at the hotel last night, for example, was beyond the call of duty."

"Not at all," the scientist protested. "It was my distinct pleasure. I truly am delighted to have you here with us, Ian."

"The pleasure's mine," I responded somewhat vacantly.

I was pretty sure that, astute as he was, Nathan detected my distractedness but he politely reserved comment. That was until I actually solicited some comment from him.

I knew we were supposed to talk business, but after hearing Nathan speak so endearingly about his upbringing and past at brunch, my mind had shifted to a more philosophical and personal plane. I seldom had a chance to talk with anyone about matters that were important to me, and this was a man I felt so comfortable talking with and whose opinion I valued. I just couldn't pass up this opportunity to discuss some of the thoughts I'd recently been having about my life.

"Nathan," I began, "We've known one another now for the better part of a year and God knows I find you one of the most perceptive people I've met. In fact, colleagues at Medicon whom I've worked with for the past nine years, who've broken bread in my home, who've attended retreats with me over the years, these people have no idea who Ian Archer is as a person. And recently I've begun to suspect that they really don't care. With you, on the other hand, I sense a genuine interest in getting to know who I am." I paused for a moment to find the right words. "I've witnessed you interacting with others. You peel away all of the fabricated exteriors and seek out the essence that uniquely defines the individual. So, if you don't mind me asking, Nathan, tell me what it is about business these days that has left so many of us bereft of trust or compassion?"

With a look that seemed to have predicted the question, Nathan replied, "My friend, I appreciate your confidence in me in by asking such a question and I hope you understand that, like you, I am only a student of life. That said, I'd suggest that the problem of which you speak is not confined to the impersonality of the business world but rather is a portrait of society in general."

I disagreed and so challenged him, "But how can this be? I've given the subject considerable thought over the past several months and have reflected on the fact that I never experienced such apathy when I was growing up as a child, nor can I ever remember feeling this way in university. And, even today, I'm reminded of our humanity on occasion through people such as yourself."

"Of course you are," my traveling companion assured me. "I didn't mean to infer that pandemic social decay is inevitable. In fact, far from it. For as long as we have dreams, we carry hope. And hope is the foundation of our future. Hope for our children, hope for our environment, hope for our welfare, hope for our love, hope for our humanity. It transcends cultures and differences and enables humans to care enough to work together, to share and to be vulnerable."

"Then what of the lack of trust and compassion that I've witnessed in so many people of late?" I added.

"People like this are so overwhelmed with the need to impress others that they've become remiss in their responsibilities to themselves," Nathan suggested.

Quizzically, I took the next step in logic, "So you are saying that they need to impress themselves?"

"Exactly!" he offered triumphantly.

Now, I consider myself to be reasonably intelligent and have often been proud of my ability to be logical in trying situations, but at that moment I felt completely lost.

"Please help me here, professor," I pleaded.

"Certainly." Nathan paused and then began deliberately, "Ask yourself how you are impressed by your own actions. I believe you'll find that when you achieve or exceed your goals, regardless of what they are, you feel good about yourself. When we have dreams that we wish to fulfill, we establish goals for ourselves and we direct our behavior towards the attainment of those goals. Hope is a constant companion on these personal journeys. And when we fulfill our dreams, our feelings of satisfaction are further validated by the world around us, including our colleagues, friends, spouses, children and so on. In essence, when we receive praise from those around us we, in turn, feel good about ourselves and reciprocate these good feelings to our own community of family and friends." Nathan stopped for a moment to make sure I was grasping what he was saying. When I nodded, he continued.

"Now, if this makes sense, then the reverse should likewise be true. If we are too caught up with life to allow ourselves to reach, to seek, to strive, and to dream in an effort to fulfill our essential personal needs, then we cease being effective life managers. Our internal compass or soul, if you will, becomes starved for growth and in such a deprived state it is reasonable to expect decay of humanity, ethics, honesty, and trust. For if one can't trust oneself, or be honest to one's own needs, or even respect one's expressions of vulnerability and compassion, then how can one exhibit these behaviors towards those around them? The result of this starved soul is the insular, self-absorbed society of which you speak."

With the picture beginning to take shape in my mind, I inquired, "So what's your prognosis for society?"

After a moment of contemplation, Nathan answered, "In a word, good. As you pointed out, I try to take the time to understand people's true nature. Often, I find that many people are well-intentioned but through their particular circumstances have become self-absorbed and consequently have lost their sense of community."

"And why do you feel that a sense of community is important?" I asked. "Don't you believe that the loner in society can still offer honesty and integrity in their everyday interactions with others?"

"Why, of course, Ian. But remember we are making generalizations here and, generally speaking, humans are social animals with an inherent need for interaction with others. And it's through this interaction that we acquire new knowledge about ourselves and our world. Community lends us strength and challenges us to consider others and in so doing helps us to grow as people. In my limited experiences, I've found that many people today have become so preoccupied with material acquisition and the preservation of their egos that little time if any is left for interaction with or consideration of the broader community. And usually these people are completely unaware of what has happened until they reach an age when they can afford to stop running all the time. Then they realize that there exists an emptiness to their lives, a hunger, an incomprehensible pain at the core of their beings. Many in Western society have coined the phrase "mid-life crisis" to capture and characterize these feelings, but I believe it can occur at any point in adult life."

"And so what is this pain, Nathan?" I asked anxiously.

With a calm, almost serene voice, he answered, "It's their soul crying out from the darkness, pleading for freedom from the mediocrity of life. They are anxious for fulfillment. They want to feel whole."

Several moments of silence passed. I gazed out the window of our car to conceal my watery eyes. Speeding by the pastoral English countryside, I found myself deeply affected by my conversation with Nathan, yet, with the help of the peaceful scenery before me, was able to compose myself.

"So what's the prescription for that?" I asked, hopeful for an answer.

"I suspect many could probably benefit from a good dose of peaceful time for meditation and contemplation, but beyond that I am sure it varies depending on the person. In fact, remember the 'loner' you spoke of earlier?" Nathan asked.

"Yes."

"Well," he continued, "that person may feel very complete in their life through community service, or hobbies, or pets, or the arts, etc, and may in fact be very engaged with the broader community in these or other spiritually fulfilling ways. They just choose a more private or personal way to connect with their community."

"So, it's by connecting to community that one's void is filled?" I asked.

"That's my belief. I have seen it happen with literally dozens of colleagues, friends and family members over the past ten years or so," Nathan answered. "But that's not to say their lives are complete. Soul work is a dynamic process, Ian, that evolves to reflect the maturity and experiences of the individual. With each new relationship we are blessed with, there are a host of new feelings, thoughts and knowledge that enhance our life and create new opportunities for growth.

"Fascinating," I responded simply. The conversation was becoming too emotional for me to carry on for much longer. As it turned out, my interruption left a gap in the conversation. When we resumed, Nathan sensitively took the initiative to turn our thoughts to work. He began to recite our Sunday afternoon agenda, followed by an overview of the research program currently underway at Biocodon in Oxford and at the satellite laboratories in Europe and Canada. Half an hour later, we were entering the city and soon thereafter were immersed in a scientific discussion.

After a hastily consumed dinner hosted by Nathan and his wife, Helen, we left this part of the country behind us and raced for our 9:30 p.m. departure out of Heathrow for Geneva.

Over the course of the days that followed, I continued to enjoy Nathan's company as we traversed the globe—from London to Geneva, then off to Hamburg and Lisbon, followed by a long flight to Buenos Aires and two days later into Santiago. The unusual warmth cast on South America at this time of year was a stark but welcome contrast to the cool and damp spring we'd experienced in Europe. The weather wasn't the only contrast on this trip, though, as our business of plant inspections and meetings in Argentina and Chile was worlds away from the leisure hours we spent there exploring wonderful eateries and engaged in provocative conversation.

The hours I spent with Nathan never seemed burdensome and our respect for each other's business acumen grew during this time. I was continuously impressed by his easygoing style and honesty. It was a refreshing change from North American corporate culture. Our shared passion for the truth forged a strong bond of trust between us, allowing me to discuss with him many of the daily struggles I'd endured of late. Obviously, aware of my responsibilities to my employer, I insisted and Nathan understood that many of my discussions were intentionally fabricated examples of situations similar to those I was dealing with at work. I hoped Nathan would offer his opinion on how to approach these issues. He never disappointed me.

On one occasion, while enjoying a glass of Chilean red wine at the end of a long, mentally arduous day, I happened to mention to Nathan my chance encounter with Karl

Lawrence several weeks earlier at my favorite new cafe. I explained Karl's parting comment, "Ian Archer, what is your pain?" and my subsequent consideration of this haunting question. Nathan reacted to my anecdote with a wry smile, as though I were speaking about someone with whom he'd shared a fraternal oath and who'd offered me an initiation invitation or a rite of passage into some secret society.

"I'm pleased that my life's hurdles bring you such joy," I said with my usual dry humor.

"On the contrary, good man," he began, "my smile is my less than subtle way of showing appreciation for the journey that lies ahead of you."

"And where is this journey going to take me?" I inquired.

"That's so much less important than the journey itself, Ian. The decisions that you'll make, the growth you'll experience within, the extraordinary people you'll meet, and the things that you'll do are each going to enrich your life immeasurably."

I qualified Nathan's comments, "That is, if I choose to embark."

Nathan was enjoying this repartee or at least his expression suggested that when he prophesized, "Oh, Ian, you've already begun. I've heard your words and seen your passion to challenge yourself and to grow. I'm excited that you've found a mentor in Karl to help you to build your future."

"But, I don't even know the man. I surely can't be mentored by someone I don't know," I argued.

"Trust in your own intuition, Ian. If you feel comfortable in speaking with this man, then embrace the opportunity. If not, then others will offer you counsel on your journey. Just don't forget that the person you shut out of your life today may be the beacon your soul is seeking tomorrow."

The wine had taken the edge off my otherwise anxious disposition. For a moment my thoughts wandered. I was a forty-three-year-old husband and father who was an executive within a major medical firm. I had friends, family, few financial concerns, and a stable job. And here I was sitting with a brilliant scientist and businessman in a wonderful Chilean hotel enjoying a superb domestic wine. How bad could things be?

For a brief moment, while lounging in generously proportioned upholstered chairs the color of dark rubies, I found peace. Not simply a feeling of relaxation that one experiences after sitting down with a drink after a long day, but rather a systemic freedom from the insane pace of the world. My mind was quieted, my soul was nourished. In this state of tranquility, I let slip my guard and allowed myself to be vulnerable.

"So," I began, "What do you suspect pains me, Nathan?"

"What I believe is not important, Ian. I'm sure you understand that. But think about it for a minute. Think about those things in your life that you feel compromise who Ian Archer is, or who Ian Archer wants to be."

With this response, Nathan stood up and added, "It's getting quite late and tomorrow we depart for Asia, so if you'll excuse me, I'm going to retire for the evening. Good night."

"Of course, Nathan," I stammered, completely unaware of the time, "Good-night, and thank you for the conversation."

"The pleasure is always mine, my friend," Nathan said as he headed off to his room.

I chose to finish the remnants of the bottle of wine we'd been sharing before packing it in for the night. Nathan's words left their usual acidic residue in my mind, making sleep an impossibility for the moment anyway. Like the unwitting bear resolved to get honey from the hive, I found myself with thoughts swarming about my head as I sought an answer to what pained me. My work life provided much fodder for contemplation, as did my relationship with Catherine, my family connections, and my feelings of community and life purpose. But these same thoughts had come in and out of my head for the past several months without resolution. I needed to channel my thoughts. I needed to assail each issue, breaking it down into its basic elements in order to understand my pain. Pleased with myself for having reached this revelation and too tired and inebriated to focus any further, I committed myself to seeking Nathan's help the following day.

As planned, I found my traveling companion in the hotel restaurant at 7:30 a.m.. I was surprised to see that his rather dapper business attire had been relegated to his suitcase in favor of what appeared to be a casual safari outfit. The contrast with my own appearance was marked and warranted an explanation.

"Good morning, Ian," Nathan volunteered with an outstretched hand. "I presume that you missed the morning news."

"Why, yes I did Nathan but how did..."

"Your suit gave you away," he explained before I could finish. "It seems as if a severe tropical storm has gripped the South Pacific. I checked with the airlines and the airport, and our flight to Singapore has been indefinitely postponed. So, I thought it would be rather civilized and appropriate to enjoy a day of relaxation and retreat. Hence my attire."

I took a moment to digest this information. With no way to get to Singapore, then Tokyo would be out of the picture as well. Given that there was no contingency for delays on this trip, this meant that our grueling seven days of travel and meetings in six countries was now over. I was relieved and mildly elated. I was tired of the pace of our travels, but extremely impressed by all that I had seen. It was obvious that Biocodon was prepared for global growth and my report to Medicon's executive would strongly recommend proceeding with the alliance.

"Nathan, I'm sorry that we won't have an opportunity to view your operations in Singapore and Tokyo, but I've been extremely pleased with the other sites visited and you can rest assured that I'll convey that to Medicon's executive committee. As for today, I'd be pleased to join you in a bit of exploration," I added.

"Splendid all 'round,'" he responded.

Following a satisfying breakfast, I changed my clothes befitting our amended itinerary, and Nathan began to usher me from one location to another. He was seeking the perfect gift for his wife. I suggested that perhaps one of the surrounding villages might prove more suitable and, with that thought, we hired a local driver and were soon beyond the limits of Santiago.

Colorful pottery appeared to be a favorite of local artisans and Nathan and I both yielded to their insistent sales pitches. Several purchases later we stopped at a hillside town and enjoyed a light lunch. Times like these always seemed so surreal to me when I allowed my mind to slip back to life in Chicago. Nathan, too, often appeared lost in the moment. We informed the driver that we wished to walk off our lunch, so without argument he tipped his hat down over his brow and reclined in the car's front seat as the two of us, reddened by our few days of South American sun, proceeded to wander about the local hillside.

Recalling my thoughts from the evening before, I engaged Nathan yet again in my quest for truth.

"Nathan," I began, "After you retired for the evening last night I ruminated over some of the things you had said."

"And what did you conclude?" he asked with a bemused smile.

"Well, that's just it. I couldn't draw any conclusions. The same general streams of thought always recur without any obvious pattern. Something I did discover last night, though, was the fact I think I've been overanalyzing things. I need to get to the basic issues."

"Very good, Ian," my mentor suggested without even a hint of condescension. "I suspect that you'll find that most, if not all, of your life challenges can be distilled into one key point."

We stopped walking at the peak of a grass-covered hill, sat, and admired the view. Before us lay rolling countryside interrupted only by clumps of trees, and the occasional farmhouse. With a cloudless blue sky, the image was perfect. While seated, I continued, "I've noted over the past week, Nathan, that you seem to speak from considerable experience on the matters that plague me. Have you found yourself in my situation before?"

"Yes, my friend, as I told you some days ago, I believe that most people find themselves searching their souls at some point in their lives. Usually it's prompted by a crisis of some sort that allows them the time to stop and to think about themselves and their world. For me, it happened ten years ago. I was a confident, successful laboratory director with a lovely wife, two children, and the promise of tenure at Oxford. Then, within a two-month period my research program fell into jeopardy due to changing priorities at the granting council and my daughter, who was seven at the time, fell deathly ill with meningitis. The strain on me and my relationship with Helen was unbearable at times. We went to a brilliant family therapist who helped us both through that period in our lives and coincidentally opened both of us up to ourselves and to each other. Even long after my daughter's health had returned and the grant's officer had recognized the error of his ways, Helen and I continued to attend workshops on spiritual exploration and development. Not that either of us had ever been particularly ardent church-goers. But, intuitively, we have always found ourselves to share a profound connection. As I have told Helen on countless occasions, 'Our spirits dance together'."

"What do you mean by that?" I interjected.

"I believe one's spirit is the intangible essence of their life," he began, " a composite of their needs, beliefs and emotions. It's that part of ourselves that recognizes a Supreme Being has designed a master plan for us. It's that part of us that seeks to define our purpose within that plan and to fulfill those roles. And when one's spirit interacts with another's or encounters new knowledge from elsewhere, it extracts this information, processes it, and feeds it to one's soul. The soul is enriched as a result. This is how Helen and I feel towards one another. Each moment together our spirits are in harmony and our souls are nourished."

"I don't think that I've ever heard spirituality described in such a compelling way. But I'm curious. How did you get from the therapist's office to the type of spiritual union you have described," I asked.

"Time," was Nathan's answer. "I truly needed to find time to invest in myself for I knew that all of my other relationships and insecurities would not mend until I mended myself. So I took time everyday——an hour of meditation. Sometimes just sitting in a quiet darkened room of the house with soft music, other times I would go for a peaceful walk alone and contemplate my challenges in my head. Regardless, I would always have a small notepad with me to record my mental meanderings. And I read a number of books on various aspects of soulfulness and self-development and love, not to blindly adopt every theory put forward, but rather to analyze the thoughts of others to determine whether they held value for me. Sometimes it helped, sometimes it didn't, but I found that this period of several months proved to be a watershed in my life. Of course, Helen was also engaged in her own process of self-discovery and healing at the time, and we supported each other on our respective journeys. And in the process, we began a new journey together as a couple. Not that either of us could have said that anything was particularly abhorrent about our relationship before that time, but we were both victimized by life, attending to matters we thought to be important. Later, we learned independently how much of what was truly important to us had been taken for granted, like our family's health, and our love, and our community of friends. The changes we've made over the past decade have brought us both immeasureable happiness and peace. But it all started with taking the time to work things out in our own minds."

I sat there on that rural Chilean hillside overwhelmed by my friend's incredible wisdom and experience. Looking out on the horizon, I felt moved, and for the first time in a long time, hopeful for myself. I thanked Nathan for sharing his story and I could feel that he was aware of my genuine gratitude. After some time of quiet reflection, we descended the hill, walked back to the car, and instructed our sleepy driver to return to the city.

6

The Awakening

The return flight back to Chicago gave me a chance to begin plotting out the changes I wished to make in my life. I allowed myself to go over in detail the events of the previous week. Thinking about my wonderful discussions with Nathan refreshed me much like the forceful spray from the shower nozzle on my sleepy morning face. Forgotten promises and antique regrets were washed from my mind. I decided to write down some key recollections, so I removed my journal from my briefcase, flipped to a blank page, dated it, and began.

Sunday March 28, 1999

Dreams

Hopes

Goals

Soul

Accomplishment

Community

Spiritual Discovery

Contemplation Meditation

Dancing Spirits

Investment in Time

I spent hours in deep reflection, carefully contemplating each of the words that appeared on the page in front of me. Writing them down enabled me eventually to see and understand their interrelationships. Like a ligament connecting one limb to another, I found the images connected with one another gracefully. I traveled back through my experiences, both painful and pleasurable, and found that all of them were instructive in one way or another. I searched within myself for the common denominator that Nathan had spoken of, for the simple truth that had evaded my life for so many years. What was missing in my life? What was my pain? Why was I denying myself peace? I closed my eyes to shut out the world of coffee-serving flight attendants, crinkling newspapers, and suits exchanging stock tips. I resolved to spend as much time as I could on this flight home contemplating these mysteries.

I began by seeking out a fundamental truth. I reasoned that the essence of every living being is the soul. It is our ethereal vessel of faith and passion and love. It evolves constantly, growing with new experiences and new knowledge. Fulfilling the soul's lifelong appetite for discovery is the responsibility of the spirit. Whether challenged by fear or inspired by hope, the spirit allows each of us to flirt with dreams, to seek new ways of being. It animates us to help others, to be better people, to find peace with ourselves in the world. Our spiritual goals involve the most intimate aspects of our lives.

At this point my mind was swirling with both Nathan's words and my own thoughts, but I pushed through these and the mental blocks of my past into uncharted territory. I came to see that our spirituality is the keystone defining and distinguishing who we are within our world, balancing the forces of love, forgiveness, morality, humanity and divinity in perfect unison. The strength of our spiritual framework determines the type and extent of support we seek from the world around us. Nourishment and encouragement from our friends and family, fulfillment from acknowledgment of our achievements, and rejuvenation from meditation and contemplation are each basic elements of the human experience and are thus needs of the spirit.

I was beginning to see things more clearly now. It was apparent to me that those who recognize but fail to attain these basic needs quickly find surrogates. In other words, the soul is expert in discriminating between a contrived feeling and the genuine article. Consequently, such individuals are restless, often feeling adrift and incomplete. When we are connected to our spirits, though, we find the capacity to understand ourselves and to experience a new level of intimacy with our own needs and with those of others. That's it, I thought. Our spirit nourishes our Soul. This sudden insight was liberating to me. I finally understood what Nathan meant when he said our spirits let us dance with others, experience newness, trust and share and explore the limits of ourselves with others. This "connectivity" is found only in certain relationships, only with those who share with us an almost familial comfort. These are our kindred spirits.

"Wow," I thought. "This stuff's amazing." I kept on thinking, stretching my mind. I really wanted some answers. I continued!

Feeling safe in the free expression of our soul enables us to stretch the limits of our vulnerability. We become empowered when we recognize the one with whom we can expand our spiritual universe, the one whose life force endows us with the energy to challenge the boundaries of our souls, to achieve new levels of awareness and achievement and growth. This, I thought, this must be what has been described as a soul mate. Soul mates must be the spiritual embodiment of synergy. They must expand the context of the soul and what it means to be whole. Soul mates open us up; they stretch the horizons of our soul, encouraging us to think differently and to view the world from a spiritual perspective, not one driven by ego or arrogance.

Soul mates... kindred spirits... Thinking about these things excited, satisfied and energized that part of me that had echoed empty for so long. Yet, despite feeling so invigorated I wondered how realistic these thoughts were and whether they were actually attainable. My mind was buzzing, but all of this thinking along with the usual exhaustion of a long flight had worn me out and I soon fell into a deep sleep.

My fatigue was clearly more profound than I had imagined, for I couldn't recall the flight attendant raising my seat in preparation for landing in Houston. When we touched down, however, I was sufficiently jolted into waking up. My immediate reaction was to try to rationalize where I was and how I got there. Moments earlier, I had been immersed in thought as a consequence of the spiritual voyage Nathan had launched in me over the previous week. Soul mates. Hmmm... That was the last thought that went through my mind before I had drifted off to sleep. Suddenly, in the here and now, I realized how much I missed my wife. Not simply over the past week, but for what seemed to me to be years. I was genuinely glad to be returning home and anxious to speak with Catherine. With these thoughts, I gathered my jacket and briefcase and prepared to change planes for the final leg of my journey. I expected to arrive home by seven thirty in the evening, providing my flight was on time and that traffic from O'Hare to Deerborne wasn't too congested. The night before, I had spoken with Catherine briefly to inform her of my change in plans and to tell her that I'd likely have dinner on the flight so she and Kyle should go ahead without me. She seemed particularly pleased that I'd soon be home. With the comfort of that knowledge, I nestled into the contours of my seat and relaxed on my Houston-Chicago flight, anxious to embrace my loved ones within just a few hours.

The flight held no disappointments, arriving promptly. Even the traffic that night from the airport was reasonable, allowing me to pull into the driveway ten minutes before my expected arrival. Struggling through the front door with a garment bag over my shoulder, a suitcase in one hand, and a briefcase in the other, I announced my arrival with a thump as everything dropped to the floor. Catherine and Kyle came running downstairs to greet me, with Kyle in the lead coming up to me and giving me a great big bear hug. The sight of Catherine, with her smiling face and her unassuming beauty evoked an emotional response in me that was quite unexpected. Never before had I returned from a trip and greeted my wife with tears in my eyes. I pulled her towards me, wrapped my arms around her, as she did likewise, and for several minutes we held each other there in the foyer of our home. Kyle, a bit uncomfortable at the sight of our affection, grabbed my garment bag and wrestled it upstairs to my bedroom. Meanwhile, Catherine and I continued to hold one another and kiss. I can't accurately convey in words the feeling of holding my wife against my body at that moment. I had missed feeling her breath on my ear, her chest moving together with my own, and her hands gently caressing my back and shoulders. I caressed her in return, seeking assurances that each part was where it belonged. Our passion for each other was undeniable, but Kyle was growing impatient for an overview of my trip, so Catherine and I would have to wait.

As I kissed her again, she saw my tears by now half way down my cheeks and, looking into my eyes asked, "Ian, why the tears, is everything all right?"

Wiping away the evidence, I smiled and said, "Everything's gonna be fine. This trip was enlightening for me, and I want to tell you everything, but first let's go see Kyle and wait to talk until he's gone to sleep."

Returning the smile, Catherine picked up my briefcase and touched my face with her delicate hand, adding "Ian Archer, I love you."

Hearing those simple words comforted me, but thinking back on that moment now I can honestly say that Catherine hadn't just comforted me; she had made my soul smile.

I tossed my suitcase next to the other bag in my bedroom and joined Kyle who was sitting on the floor of his room reading through a National Geographic book on South America in anticipation of a thorough overview of my trip. He loved to hear about my travels. He wanted to know what the countries were like, where they were on his globe, what the people and food were like, and anything else I could tell him. He pushed the large leather-bound publication over on the floor to make room for my outstretched frame, but I sat up next to him instead to prevent the enticement of sleep from grabbing hold of me too soon. Within twenty minutes Catherine, who had emptied my suitcases and started the laundry, joined us. A half-hour later our son, the intrepid explorer, had fallen off to sleep.

We hated to wake him up just to get ready for bed, but he was now too big for us to get him into his pj's and lift him into bed on our own. Zombie-like he put on his bed clothes and bleary-eyed but content crawled into bed and managed to get a 'g'night' out before he drifted off again. We kissed him and quietly retreated from his room. I told Catherine that I'd join her in a few minutes after I'd cleaned up and within minutes I was enjoying a revitalizing shower.

I found Catherine in the living room curled into a ball in the corner of the sofa with a bottle of wine and two glasses within reach on the end table. Before getting our drinks, I crawled up next to her and kissed her waiting lips.

Then, pouring the wine, I asked, "How was your week, love?"

"Busy," she started, "But otherwise uneventful. Kyle had two hockey games and practices as well as baseball practice yesterday. Things were quiet in the office, though, so I managed everything. Thanks for the flowers and chocolates by the way. I know I don't always acknowledge you for thinking about me when you're out of town, but every time a delivery arrives at the office I feel as if you're with me, here in my heart."

"You're welcome," I replied as I handed Catherine her glass. "You know I appreciate everything you do, especially the extra load you put up with when I'm away. Let me propose a toast. To my beautiful wife, to our love, and to the promise of a wonderful future together."

"Thanks, Ian. I will drink to that." With a quizzical look, she probed further, "So, tell me, what happened on your trip?"

"Well, from a business perspective, everything was fine. The research program at Biocodon is wonderful and very efficient. Their clients in Lisbon and Buenos Aires were very supportive and the manufacturing operations in Santiago were surprisingly state-of-the-art. I'm convinced we should go ahead with the alliance."

"That's wonderful, Ian, but there was more to your trip than that, wasn't there?" she inquired searchingly.

I knew that my face revealed subtle changes in my disposition. My emotions at the door, my prolonged hug, even my voice carried inflections that betrayed my emotional state despite my best efforts to conceal it.

I continued, "Yes, Catherine, I had a great week with Nathan Currie. We've become good friends. He shared many of his life experiences with me and, in the process, helped me to understand why I've been feeling tormented for so long."

Catherine had met Nathan on one prior occasion at a cocktail reception hosted by Medicon during his last visit to Chicago some five months earlier. I remember her impression of him because it was so out of keeping for her. She remarked about how comfortable it was to speak with him, that she felt he was genuinely interested in what she thought, and that he was highly intuitive. For someone usually reserved when meeting a stranger, Catherine was unusually at ease with Nathan.

"I can understand that," she replied anxiously, "He's a very open and aware man. What I don't understand is what he could've possibly said that helped you so much when all of my attempts over the years have been futile. This is the first time you've admitted to me that you've been tormented, Ian, even though I've sensed this in you for a long time now. It seems as if you've experienced an epiphany or something."

"I know, Catherine, I know. Please don't be offended. I don't know exactly why Nathan was able to help me see things that I couldn't before. Maybe it's a timing thing. Maybe I'm in a better place now to think things through than I was before. Who knows? But the way you've described it as an epiphany is right on, Catherine." I responded slowly as if asking for her forgiveness. "I feel that I have gotten in touch with my spiritual self again."

I could see that she was pleased by my openness. It was clear that she wanted to pursue our conversation, but I knew I couldn't do it justice in the hour or so that I might be able to stay awake. Therefore I asked of her, "Love, I know you want to talk about this and I'm eager to share my thoughts with you, but I'm very, very tired mentally. I don't intend to go to the office tomorrow, because I have more work to do before the executive meeting on Wednesday. Besides, they're not expecting me back until then anyway. This is very important for us, though. Could you possibly leave work early tomorrow, say at noon or one, so we could have a few hours together before Kyle gets home?"

She understood my fatigue and agreed to put off our discussion until the following afternoon. With a somewhat disappointed expression, she added, "Are you really that tired?"

Completely aware of her emotions at that moment, I repeated, "Sweetheart, I said that I am mentally fatigued. I've missed you so much this past week that an army couldn't stop me from making love with you tonight."

With that, we went upstairs to our room where within moments our passion was engaged and my promise was fulfilled.

It was 9:30 a.m. Monday morning before I woke. After showering and putting on jeans and a T-shirt, I went downstairs to the kitchen where a thoughtful little note was left for me next to the coffee pot. It read, "My love, thank you for last night. I look forward to our rendezvous this afternoon. Until then, know my thoughts are with you. Always, Catherine." The note warmed my heart as I prepared and ate my breakfast.

I took my coffee into the living room where I could feel the morning sun streaming through the windows. Grabbing my agenda and a notepad, I sat down and carefully rewrote my schematic about the "Soul" , this time embellishing the collection of words with lines and arrows in an attempt to unify the image.

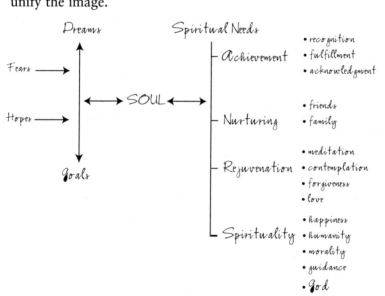

As each word formed on the page, I felt as if I'd added vigor to a new life. Every thought was carefully chosen, its placement considered with anatomical precision. Life was breathed into my creation when each piece of my original skeletal schematic was fleshed out and shown to be inextricably linked to the Soul. I reviewed my work like a proud father.

Contemplating my recent revelations and, more importantly, what they meant for me in a practical sense, I wondered how my desire to be spiritually engaged, to dispel the superficialities of life, and to truly focus on the needs that nourished my soul would affect my relationship with Catherine. I thought about my work. In the context of Wednesday's upcoming executive meeting, when my report and recommendations on the investigation would be presented, I questioned whether my analysis of the situation had been fair. Maybe I had taken a biased position despite the evidence Karen and Paul had gathered, merely to protect my own interests? Once started, I found it difficult to hold back the thoughts. I mentally revisited the period four years earlier when my mother was ill. Why did I continue to harbor guilt around my mother's passing? Surely such feelings were unfounded, but still I found myself evaluating these emotions as if I were a third person arbitrating the situation. What was it that allowed me to feel this way? I didn't arrive at an answer, however, before the next attention-seeking thought entered my mind. I considered my relationships with family members, my father, my sister and brother, Kyle, and Catherine's parents. Were these people aware of how much I loved them, or had I allowed other issues to compromise my telling them? And what of our friends? For the past nine years as a couple we had developed few true friendships. Not at all like our days out on the West Coast where our lives were enriched by interacting with a diverse group of people.

Feeling somewhat overwhelmed with thought, I got up, grabbed a sweater, and stepped out onto the back deck. I took in several deep breaths of fresh air. Although the sun was full in the midday sky and was providing warmth on my face, the ambient temperature still struggled to reach sixty degrees. Leaning on the railing, I allowed my senses to soak up the surroundings. Cardinals and starlings played in the trees creating a symphony of sound. The spruce and pine trees that bordered my back yard provided a healthy green and bluish backdrop to the deciduous species that would soon display leaves and flowers of green and red and yellow and white. The splashing of the brook, filled with winter run-off, provided a counterpoint to the birds, and I could tell a neighbor's efforts in the kitchen would soon be rewarded as something sweet-smelling was carried on a light breeze to my location. I sat down on a plastic deck chair and closed my eyes. My face was caressed by the wind and my cheeks blushed warmly in response. I felt at peace. This was my epiphany, as Catherine had called it the night before. I wanted to be able to close my eyes and find peace in my heart with the knowledge that my soul's needs were being met and that each day I was striving to grow spiritually. I wanted to feel whole. I hungered for the fellowship of friends and family. I wanted to dream, to set goals and to achieve them. I wanted to bring who I was as a spiritual being into my workplace and to cultivate an environment of respect and trust and humanity. I wanted my first thought every morning and my last thought each night to be one of celebration for the gift that God had given me in my wife and my son. And I wanted to share the feeling with Catherine of our spirit's dancing together.

With the breeze picking up, I was beginning to get cool so I returned inside and took a minute to write my thoughts down. I found that this journey of discovery I was embarking upon was that much clearer in my mind when I committed it to words on the page. I was almost finished when the phone rang. Catherine had called to tell me she was on her way and would be home in twenty minutes. It was 1:15 p.m.. I made a light lunch for the two of us and finished writing in my agenda.

With Catherine's arrival, I jumped to the door, helped her with her coat, and wrapped my arms around her waist as we kissed. My immediate instinct was to escort her up to our room to resume our passion of the night before, but instead I thanked her for the note, kissed her again, and led her into the kitchen to break bread with me. Our conversation was interrupted by several kisses and our hands found each other's on the table throughout our lunch. I suspected our feelings of intimacy for one another were heightened by our recent prolonged separation. Regardless, I loved the way I was feeling and the way Catherine was responding to me.

After a twenty-minute lunch we took our tea into the living room where I'd abandoned my notes.

As I paused to sip some tea, Catherine asked impatiently, "What's up?"

"You know I've been distracted with work lately," I began.

"More than just lately, Ian," she corrected. "It's been months, even years since I've seen the guy I once knew."

"I know. I know. I've been thinking about it a lot lately. When Scott left the company something left with him. It's never been the same since. Then Mom died. And rather than do as you did and take the time then to reflect on what's important in my life, I buried myself in my work," I confessed in a half-apologetic tone.

Catherine nodded in agreement, adding " ...And when

Stoner took over, it wasn't long before questionable ethics became standard operating procedure. I witnessed some morally repugnant behavior myself. Like the way Tod Slater made rude remarks to many of the women at the Christmas party last year and how he and some of his people shamelessly adulterated the barbequed pig at the picnic a few years ago. Slimy cretins! I guess I wondered what compelled you to stay there. We aren't exactly cash-starved after all. I've really tried to understand what your motivation could be, as I'm sure you know that people conclude 'you are the company you keep,' and in this case, that ain't good."

"As much as I don't want to admit it, I think it's been a combination of things. Apathy, denial, and the lure of executive perks and privileges."

"I'm not sure I follow…"

"Well, first Scott has heart trouble relatively early in life and, before I know it, he has left and in his place is a guy that's the antithesis of my mentor in every way. I try to tell myself that it doesn't matter, that I just need to do my job to the best of my ability, but I'm constantly faced with one change after another that chokes out the last breaths of enthusiasm that I once had for my job. Then Mom gets sick and for the next three years we ride an emotional roller coaster through the peaks and valleys of her illness doing what we can to assist her and Dad. Then the news came that mom had died. I know that at the time I felt as if a part of me died along with her. I saw you mourning in your way through prayer and meditation and reading. In a way I felt envious of you for that. But another part of me felt I needed to be strong for you and for Kyle. Inside, I was being ripped apart by all kinds of indescribable emotions. I sought refuge in my work. I know that I should've talked with you, sweetheart, but I rationalized to myself that being vulnerable would compromise my responsibility to be strong for you and Kyle. So, I buried myself in work. Then I was promoted. And things once so important to me, no longer were. It's taken my recent feelings of inadequacy at work and this whole investigation for me to see clearly how I too have become a casualty of Medicon's compromised principles." I paused to sip my tea and to allow Catherine an opportunity to say something.

Tears filled her eyes, " I'm sorry, Ian. I'm so sorry. I should've been more supportive."

"And I should've trusted you with my emotions. The therapist we saw five years ago hinted at this, but I ignored her," I admitted. Taking my wife's hand in mine I continued, "Catherine, this isn't about finding fault. It's about recognizing that something's been wrong and wanting to change that for the better."

We talked on. Our honesty with each other that afternoon was wonderfully cathartic. We discovered that we had many common concerns and grievances, but over the years had never taken the time to share our thoughts. We reflected on the relationships with friends and family that we had allowed to deteriorate since our move to Chicago nine years before. Catherine came to understand that although I enjoyed my work and the team in my department, I felt that the culture at Medicon had become cold, unethical and insensitive to the very people the company professed to recognize as its most important asset. It was the first time Catherine heard me admit how Harold Stoner regarded my principles as antique sentiments. She easily understood how that had eroded my feeling of self over time.

Similarly, I gained a better understanding from Catherine about her fears of pursuing greater contact with family.

"You must understand, Ian, I don't think I've ever

recovered from the feelings of abandonment I had as an adolescent. Between my father's ego and my mother's apathy, I was lost. I'm sure at some level this pain has compromised my abilities to draw closer to your family as well."

I listened intently, thinking that perhaps it was a combination of my own failings to maintain family ties coupled with Catherine's discomfort in doing so that cultivated my personal feelings of guilt around my mother's illness and passing. This made some sense to me and strangely I felt comforted to have gained some understanding of these emotions at last.

After wading through nearly a decade of our problems, I explained to Catherine my mental condition prior to the Biocodon trip. I reminded her of Karl Lawrence's discussion with me several weeks before and then recounted the series of conversations Nathan and I had enjoyed over the course of the previous week.

"All the while I was in Europe and South America, I was haunted by Karl's question: 'What is your pain?' 'What is your pain?' Then with Nathan's help I began to think about my life and unscramble the truth. It finally came to me one night, while sitting alone in the hotel bar nursing what must have been my fifth or sixth glass of wine. Nathan had gone off to his room nearly an hour earlier, leaving me with my thoughts. I remember writing out the phrase, 'What is your pain?' The answer didn't come. I looked closer at the words 'your pain' and separated each letter with a space. Perhaps the wine had allowed me to think more creatively because soon something became obvious to me after rearranging some of the letters. 'Your pain' now read: 'you r ian p.' You are Ian Phillippe. Was this some kind of trick that Karl had played on me? I reasoned it couldn't have been since he never knew my middle name. But when I stopped to think about the question in the context of this message, I knew that I had found my answer. My pain is that I have not been truthful to myself. I have not been who I truly am and, after years of this, I feel hollow. I want to feel like the old Ian. I want my soul to feel whole."

Although I didn't tell everything in sequence, I managed to paint a picture for Catherine of where each thought had led me in dealing with my struggle. I showed her the words in my agenda, and the diagram I had sketched. I don't think I'd ever been so vulnerable and open with my wife, but I wanted her to know what I felt. And once I started to share my truth with her, I found it was incredibly easy. It was as though one phrase pulled out the next and so on for over an hour. We smiled, even laughed, and we cried too, but we did this together and the emotions were honest and therapeutic. She was moved by my words and told me she wanted many of the same things as I, and was prepared to begin a journey with me to achieve a greater sense of inner peace and freedom. I told her I trusted her completely and wanted always to be truthful with her about my emotions, and she reciprocated these sentiments. We committed to ourselves and to each other that this would take precedence over all other external aspects of our lives until we felt peace in our lives. Emotionally exhausted, we lay down together on the couch, kissed for a time, and then fell asleep.

Four o'clock and Kyle's return from school was announced by the sound of his knapsack landing on the front porch. Catherine and I couldn't have rested for more than fifteen minutes, but it was nonetheless refreshing. After holding each other for another moment, we kissed, then got up. I grabbed a banana and pitched it to Kyle's waiting hands. He was always famished when he arrived home, but sometimes managed to focus his energies more on street hockey than on his stomach. Catherine and I started to prepare dinner, and when everything was underway, I ran upstairs to collect the souvenirs I'd purchased for Catherine and Kyle on my trip but hadn't had the chance to give them the day before.

After saying goodnight to Kyle that evening, a process that was protracted due to his profuse thanks and need for further information regarding the gifts' origins, I joined Catherine to watch some tv. While sitting there, I felt an urge to phone my father, so after the program's end, I excused myself and went to my study.

On the fourth ring the receiver was picked up, "Hello."

"Hi Dad. It's Ian. How're you doing?"

"Hi Ian. I'm well," he responded with a note of surprise. "How are you and the family?"

It had probably been two months since we'd last spoken. "We're all doing fine. I just thought I'd call to see how things were with you."

"Well that's nice of you. Remember I told you about how I was looking into a cruise? Well, I'm leaving in two days. Three weeks in the Mediterranean. With the cold we've had here this past winter, I'm really looking forward to it, son," he said with obvious excitement in his voice.

Knowing it was my dad's first vacation since mom's passing, I was very happy for him, "Well that's great. I just got back from a business trip to Europe and South America myself."

I think his level of excitement for his own trip was piqued when I described some of the sights I'd seen. "I'm proud of you, son. It sounds like your work is going along really well."

"Thanks, Dad. It has its challenges, but I'm doing my best," I explained without much detail. It didn't seem to make sense to worry him needlessly about my own problems.

"Just do what you know to be right, Ian. Then you'll find the outcome's easy to live with, no matter what it is."

Despite my few words, I'm sure he could sense my appreciation for his wisdom. "Thanks, Dad. Hey, how would it be if we came to visit for a few days after you get back from your trip?"

"That would be wonderful. I'd really like that."

"Great. Well you have a terrific time overseas and be safe. We'll be in touch after you get back. Kyle and Catherine say hello. And, Dad, I love you."

Sounding pleased to have heard from me, he conveyed his love to me generously in his own inimitable way. "I'll look forward to seeing all of you soon. Take care, son. Goodbye."

"Bye, Dad."

I hung up the phone, went upstairs and joined Catherine who was awaiting me in bed.

The next morning at the office was remarkably calm given my nine-day absence. Although my desk was piled high with reading materials, there were no crises awaiting my return and for that I was grateful. The gifts of pottery and jewelry which I'd purchased for Jackie were warmly received and prompted numerous questions about my trip which added twenty minutes to my morning briefing with her. Jackie seemed to detect a subtle change in my demeanor, as she asked if I was all right several times that morning. Others migrated to my office as well over the course of those first few hours including each of my department heads. I requested that Jackie inform Paul and Karen that I needed to meet with them at three o'clock. When asked whether the meeting was to be in my office, I suggested the cafe instead and provided directions as a reminder to them. The balance of my day was spent checking in with my staff and paring down the stacks of paper on my desk. A "make-your-day-kind-of" fax arrived for me at two-thirty. It was from Nathan, offering thanks for the previous week and letting me know that a parcel was on its way, in his words, " to help you on your journey." His thoughtfulness brought a moment of cheer into my day and I felt special that he was committed to helping me through my spiritual recovery. Soon after that at about quarter to three, I packed a few things into my briefcase including the agenda for my executive meeting the following day, as I would be leading the afternoon's session. Sensing some uneasiness in Jackie before I departed my office, I asked if she'd be home that evening to receive a phone call from me. She nodded and I smiled, wishing her a good afternoon and then left for my meeting with Karen and Paul.

Walking into the coffee house, I felt my anxieties relating to this meeting and my impending presentation for tomorrow carried away on the soothing bass notes of the blues music being played. Paul and Karen had already arrived and had found a table with four comfortable chairs. I lay my briefcase and jacket on the vacant chair after greeting my colleagues and, observing that they'd already been served, excused myself to get a coffee. On my return to the table, I quickly scouted the room, half hoping to find Karl Lawrence tucked away in some corner. Few patrons occupied the cafe, however, and Karl was not among them. Once seated, I opened my briefcase to retrieve my copy of Karen and Paul's original investigation and recommendations. I lay it on the table intentionally and noticed how it aroused my colleagues' attention. I was sure they were feeling uneasy about the conversation to follow, so I began immediately with my reasons for calling this meeting.

"Paul and Karen, I've asked you here to discuss a few things relating to the report that I'll be making to the executive tomorrow afternoon," I began.

Apparently displeased with me still, Paul interrupted, "I thought you'd made it perfectly clear to us a few weeks ago what your presentation was going to look like."

"Yes I did, Paul, but since then I've been doing a lot of soul searching. I don't want to bore the two of you with all the details, but I've been thinking about all sorts of things, like why I wanted to move my family out here nine years ago, what this company used to be, and what it has become. More importantly, however, I've come to realize that the company and more precisely its executive management has infiltrated my own spirit and led me to compromise my principles. To be honest, I've felt backed into a corner, where I've been forced to acknowledge that the best resolution is the one that's best for the executive. When I arrived at Medicon nine years ago, Scott Ashbury was president and he told me at the time that one of the things he admired about me was my independent thinking. I was not a lemming, he said. Yet, less than a decade later I find myself compromising what I know to be right, just like the others and simply to appease and protect them. Finally, I've recognized that the ethical insolvency found around the executive boardroom table has been a product of this perverse idea that each of us must relinquish our morality in order to protect the firm. I now know that Medicon would never be facing such a situation as the one you two've unearthed, had trust and respect been expected of all employees here, especially those establishing policy. I want you both to know that I am ashamed of myself, but over the past several weeks I've found an inner strength and peace in knowing that I can choose to control my actions and do something about this situation."

Karen and Paul sat in stunned silence for a few moments until Karen, in her usual timid manner, tried to console me. "Ian, we all know that it's impossible to understand the pressures that've been placed on you. We believe you are a good person, one of Medicon's best, but have been put in a really tenuous position."

I appreciated the vote of confidence, but thought to myself that this meeting wasn't about being liked by others. Ultimately, it was about liking myself.

"Thanks for the support, Karen, but what I want to tell you both is that tomorrow I intend to stand up for myself and for what is truly best for Medicon. I've reviewed your recommendations several times and I believe them to be fair. Are you both still willing to stand behind them?" I asked expecting a positive response.

I wasn't disappointed, but insisted that they think about the implications. "You see, I suspect Stoner and several others will seek retribution for my actions. That could include my own dismissal, a significant number of departmental lay-offs, and you two may also be dismissed, or at least seriously reprimanded."

Paul began, "Ian you've always been a mentor for me and, save for your decision a few weeks ago, I've always respected your judgment. What I've heard makes me proud to be a member of your team. I'm quite prepared to stand up for what I know to be right."

"Likewise, for me, Ian," Karen added.

"Very well then," I concluded with a sigh of relief. "Obviously, I'd appreciate it if you'd both keep this discussion strictly confidential."

In agreement, they shook my hand, put their jackets on, and left me feeling good about myself. I had my coffee refreshed and, as I sipped it slowly, I could hear my dad's words from the night before replay in my mind. Dad's advice was so true: doing the right thing is easy to live with.

By 4:00 p.m. I had had fifteen minutes of solitude to ponder my meeting. My thoughts were drifting elsewhere as the design of the cream in my coffee had me mesmerized. I was brought back to my surroundings by the sound of a deep and familiar voice.

"Hello, there. Ian, isn't it?"

"Yes it is. Karl, it's wonderful to see you! Please, would you join me?" I responded.

"Of course. You seem a bit distracted, though. Is everything OK?"

Smiling triumphantly, I offered, "Yes, everything's fine, thank you. In fact, I know that my life is about to benefit from some significant changes."

"How's that?" Karl asked, carefully examining my expression.

"I now know the answer to your question, Karl. I know what my pain is and, more than that, I'm beginning to do something about it."

With that, I shared my story of recent self-discovery with Karl, who seemed visibly pleased with my honesty. When I told him I wanted to feel complete as I once had, he nodded like one who had foreseen this revelation. I told him that I had sought out his company here on a few previous occasions to talk about his question, but was disappointed never to come across him. He explained that circumstances prevented him from being there as often as he wished, but that obviously his absence hadn't hindered my progress. He talked about his own experiences in life, though not on the same level I had shared with Nathan. All the same, it was comforting to know Karl could empathize with my journey. Before I knew it, the hour of five was upon us and I had to get home. I wanted to have dinner ready that night before Catherine's arrival, so I thanked Karl for the conversation and told him I hoped to see him again soon.

"You can count on it, Ian" he answered.

Later that evening, I placed the call to Jackie that I had planned earlier in the day. She understood my concerns and requests and promised her complete support. Following the call, Catherine and I sat down to talk about the decision that I'd made and the impact it might have on our family. As she reminded me, we were financially comfortable and luckily already owned our home. I was relatively young, well educated and, as she put it, "Any firm would kill to find someone like you." Her support was unequivocal and very comforting to say the least. Later, as we lay in bed, a calming sensation gently overcame me. At that moment I sensed that beyond the benefits to Catherine and myself, my spiritual awakening had the potential to be like a stone tossed in a pond, rippling its way through the lives of each of those it touched.

Regenerating the Soul

*Thought is the soul's chariot; a thoughtless man
doesn't let his soul go anywhere.*

Margaret Fishback Powers

ednesday morning at the office was no different
from any other in my nine years at Medicon
with the exception that, on that day, Jackie was
unusually quiet. I think she was trying to keep me free from
distractions, so I'd remain focused for the afternoon. I really admired this woman who helped to keep my work on an
even keel. Jackie was always truthful, loyal, and thoughtful,
if at times protective, of the division and its leader. This
morning she was wearing a brave face, for she was well

aware that what I was about to do was definitely out of step with the other executives. Regardless, she concealed her fear fairly well.

Although lunch was to be served at the meeting, I elected to review my notes instead. I was glad that I had, for at 12:15 p.m. Catherine called.

"Hello, Ian Archer speaking," I answered. Jackie had stepped out to run an errand leaving me to answer my phone directly.

"Are you nervous?" Catherine's familiar voice asked, dismissing the need for an endearing "Hello."

"Oddly enough, I'm not, Catherine. A month ago I had little to say to the executive and was very anxious, but today I'm remarkably calm. I feel an inner peace that I haven't felt in a long long time."

With genuine emotion in her voice, Catherine began, "I'm happy that you have peace in your heart, darling. I know you've wrestled with a lot over the past six months—well, longer—I know it's been years, but this time is different for both of us. I 'spose in some ways we had to experience spiritual bankruptcy and have the right people in our lives to help us to recognize that fact before we could do anything about it to make things better. Much of what you have been saying over the past few days, honey, has served as a mirror for me, one that I can hold up to my own soul. All those courses I've attended over the years in the search for personal peace and spiritual fulfillment, I guess it all rang hollow when I heard others describe their experiences because they seemed so foreign to the way we lived our lives. When similar words crossed your lips, though, I was moved by your absolute trust in me. Allowing yourself to be so vulnerable awakened me to the reality that it is safe for me to be vulnerable with you too. I'm feeling so liberated, Ian. I hear the words and the messages again, only this time the volume is turned up. Sweetheart, I just wanted to say that I am proud of what you're doing, and I stand beside you all the way — no matter where the road leads."

Catherine's sentiments made my heart swell. "Thank you, sweetheart. Your words mean a lot to me, especially right now."

"I also wanted to let you know," she continued, "that a friend from my office mentioned the name of a family therapist in Deerborne. I thought it might be a good idea to get a little information from her. Then we could talk about whether it would be worthwhile attending an introductory session."

"Sure, Catherine, that sounds great. Go for it."

"Well, I 'spose I should let you go," Catherine suggested. "I just wanted to let you know that I'm with you always."

Pleased that she had called, I told her, "I know that, darling, but hearing it straight from you means the world to me, so thank you."

"You're welcome. Please remember to call me when you return to your office after the meeting, ok? I'll be waiting to hear from you," she added.

"I will, and thanks again. G'bye." With that, I hung up, and with copies of the final report and recommendations in hand, I walked confidently down the hall to the executive boardroom.

"There he is," boomed the baritone voice of Harold Stoner as I entered the room. It was ten minutes before 1:00 p.m.. "What's with you, Ian, no lunch today? Let me guess—you're trying to preserve that girlish figure of yours?" my CEO suggested in his usual banal humor.

Did I mention that Stoner could be a poster child for gluttony? He was often seen even at work with an obnoxious cigar in one hand and a drink in the other. The irony of a man at least eighty pounds overweight and sporting several vices who was representing a major international medical firm was often too compelling for the competition to ignore. And yet Stoner seemed oblivious to the image he was portraying. This always added to the public relations challenge that my division faced.

"Good afternoon, Harold," I replied confidently. "Are we ready to begin?"

"Hell, yes," Stoner responded. "But first, let me introduce you to Valerie Fairbanks. Valerie's one of our Board members and at last week's meeting of our Board of Directors she was asked to sit in on our little executive meeting to get apprised of our emerging alliance with Biocodon. I mentioned to Val, here, that the timing was perfect given that you've just returned from a tour of their operations."

"It's a pleasure to meet you, Ms. Fairbanks," I offered. "The alliance with Biocodon is truly an exciting opportunity which I'd be pleased to share with you."

"Wonderful, Mr. Archer. I realize you've just returned and are unprepared to give a presentation at this point, but Wall Street has been hounding the Board for some strong signals of growth. So, we'd like to be able to expedite this agreement if it's in Medicon's best interests to do so," the woman explained.

Within minutes, I found myself in front of the executive and Ms. Valerie Fairbanks delivering an unrehearsed dissertation summarizing my trip, the financial arguments, Biocodon's research program, their product line, their customer's support, and their manufacturing capabilities. I was later to learn that this woman of around sixty years of age was a very successful Chicago banking executive who was renown as a pillar of the local arts community and who had some thirty-five years earlier married into one of the city's wealthiest families. She was respected by many, liked by fewer, and feared by almost all. Regardless, she seemed to be very reasonable, asking intelligent questions as I continued. I recall it was somewhere between my recounting of events in Europe and South America that I shared a glance with her and recognized that there was a potential dual purpose to her appearance there that day. Whether she was aware of it or not, I felt that my opportunity to ensure that the Board took action on my team's recommendations was staring me in the face. Yes, today there would be a reckoning.

After I finished my presentation and exhausted the audience of questions, a vote was taken as to whether or not Medicon would consummate the proposed deal. The executive overwhelmingly agreed. This pleased me and prompted me to introduce the next agenda item, the investigation.

At that moment, Stoner interrupted, "Recognizing your hectic schedule, Valerie, perhaps this'd be a good time to break for a few minutes so you can escape from the dreariness which the rest of us must endure."

"No way," I thought. I knew this was Stoner's attempt to escape Board prosecution for what he'd allowed to occur. But I wasn't going to allow that to happen. Ms. Fairbanks was not one to be ushered out before she was ready, and I was going to ensure that she felt very welcome indeed.

"In fact, Harold, my afternoon has been cleared, so if your people don't mind, I'd enjoy hearing about how the firm's operating," Valerie confidently asserted.

"I, for one, am most pleased to extend our hospitality, Ms. Fairbanks," I uttered with remarkable composure. I knew that in such a statement I'd accomplished two feats: first, by Harold Stoner's icy stare and furrowed brow, I could feel his anger with me and, second, I had tipped the first domino; now I could almost sit back and observe the cascade of reactions in my audience. On both counts, I felt a measure of satisfaction.

"Splendid, then," cheered our guest. "I thank you all. Mr. Archer, please continue."

The green flag had been waved and copies of Paul and Karen's report were being distributed. I was proud of both of them at that moment and, although they weren't there experiencing the meeting first-hand, I felt their supportive presence as two dozen anxious eyes in the room reviewed the twelve-page summary and recommendations. For the benefit of Ms. Fairbanks, I retraced the entire history of the investigation, from Paul's initial innocent exploration through company records when trying to generate a positive news release, to the financial indiscretions perpetrated by Tod Slater and many of his staff, to the inappropriate dismissals of non-compliant employees and the harassment that a number of them had experienced. My announcement of Harold Stoner's condoning of these improprieties and of his own receipt from Slater of large gifts purchased at company expense drew gasps from almost everyone present. The tension in the room was thick, to say the least. At times, I felt that if the windows could've been opened, I would've been quickly tossed out one of them. About twenty minutes into my report, I began making recommendations. The Board would be asked to handle the discipline for Harold Stoner. Otherwise, the suggestions included dismissal of Tod

Slater and his two directors, demotion of six sales managers, and the implementation of new policies for sales expenses amongst all representatives. Further, all of those who had been inappropriately dismissed or harassed would be eligible for compensation as deemed appropriate by a new company ombudsman reporting directly to the president. New zero-tolerance policies on harassment and abuse would be developed and the entire firm would be educated on their implications. I embellished my statements with a caustic message to everyone in the room regarding the executive's responsibility to establish the ethical benchmarks for the firm and how I felt that we had failed miserably in that regard. Then, I concluded with anecdotes garnered from interviews of staff throughout the firm that exemplified the lack of trust, the poor morale, and the declining productivity that had grasped the heart of Medicon.

Finally, I offered plaudits to all of those who had contributed to the investigation and most notably praised Karen and Paul for their tireless, thankless, and often disheartening efforts: "In uncovering this cancer that has metastasized throughout Medicon, these two individuals have, in my opinion, offered hope to the firm to arrest the malignancy, and to ensure Medicon's healthy future. They've acted out of concern for the firm and with the highest degree of integrity. Their motivation and principles have revealed my own inadequacies and those of the rest of this executive committee. Karen and Paul should be highly commended."

With these final words, I awaited questions. A few inquiries were made by Valerie Fairbanks, but otherwise my audience was completely silent.

Finally, Ms. Fairbanks rose, "Mr. Archer, I thank you for your report and presentation. I'll be certain to inform the Board at my earliest opportunity of the report's contents. In the meantime, I'd ask that you make yourself available to the Board over the next week or so, as I'm certain they'll require a comprehensive briefing themselves."

"Most definitely, Ms. Fairbanks. I welcome the opportunity to address the Board. And, again, many thanks for your attendance today and for your commitment to this process."

As the well-dressed, silver-haired woman exited the room with Harold Stoner at her heels, the rest of the room looked anxiously at me. A few cast congratulatory expressions in my direction, but the majority shook their heads with sorrowful looks as if viewing a fallen comrade, a victim of 'life in the real world.'

Stoner returned to the room minutes later and without hesitation bellowed, "This meeting's over! Archer, in my office, now!"

I'd expected as much and was prepared for the engagement. Calmly, I left the room and paraded past onlookers in the hallway as I made my way towards the president's palatial office. I expected the expletives which followed my arrival, but was surprised at the unprecedented creativity he used in stringing them together.

"Archer," he said after a few minutes of tirade, "your career is over. You'll be ruined throughout the industry. Where the hell do you get off reporting such nonsense in front of the old lady? I'm surprised she didn't have a stroke. And that bit about me—that's precious. How do you expect to prove your allegations without any records?"

Having foreshadowed such a reaction, I'd taken pains the day before to remove a box of files from my office and had instructed Jackie to inform Karen and Paul do likewise. Just to be safe, I'd also asked Jackie the night before to copy the files and to take them to her own home over lunch on Wednesday. From there she was to call the courier and have the box shipped to a friend and former business associate of mine for safe keeping. Thus, comfortable in my position, I allowed Stoner to continue with his threats and nervous stammering.

"Don't expect to be removing any company property from these offices until this is settled! If I had my way you'd be out of here this minute, but I'll postpone any decision until being directed by the Board. Meanwhile, you'd best keep a very low profile around here, Archer."

It was obvious that everything recorded in the investigation's report was going to be trivialized by Stoner, and I knew that that moment wasn't the time to remind the man how he'd led the firm into its present weakened state. So, with my head high, and still a strong sense of pride in what I had done, I returned to my office.

"Is everything ok, Ian," Jackie asked nervously. "People are already talking in the halls."

"Please, come into my office for a moment, Jackie," I directed her.

Inviting her to sit, I began to relay the highlights of what had just happened. When finished, I asked her, "Were you able to complete that task I'd requested of you?"

"Of course, Ian, and may I add that I think it was a smart thing to do as well."

Pleased with her support, I still felt the need to caution her. "I hope it doesn't come to such measures, but it's better to be protected than not. In any event, be prepared to have Security check your things tonight and every night until this thing is resolved."

"I will, Ian. Are you gonna be all right?" she asked with concern.

"Of course, I will. I can honestly say that this has been the finest hour of my career. And as for you, although I can't make any promises, I can tell you that if I have employment, then I'll ensure that you do as well, wherever that may be. I know that I've been remiss many times over the years in telling you how much I appreciate all that you do. I consider you a good friend, Jackie, and your strength in the past and today are an inspiration to many, including me."

With that, I suggested that she leave for the day. Meanwhile, I placed a few calls to colleagues before fulfilling my promise to Catherine to let her know the outcome of the meeting. Seeing little point in clinging to the office that afternoon, as soon as I finished speaking with my wife, I locked up, and left for the day.

It was 2:30 p.m. on the last day of March and as I sank into the driver's seat of my car I thought to myself how crazy this month had been. I hadn't had lunch and was beginning to feel hunger pangs, so decided to stop at my favorite haunt to reward myself with a little indulgence. Walking in the door, I was greeted by the aroma of freshly ground coffee beans competing with what seemed to be minestrone soup. My sense of smell proved correct, so I asked for a bowl of soup along with some dark rye bread and a coffee. I sat down at a table I'd called my own before and, accompanied this time with very soft classical orchestral sounds, I devoured my late lunch. Afterwards, while sipping my coffee, I began to contemplate the afternoon's events. My father had been right. I knew everything would work out well because my heart was at peace with my decision. I thought about Nathan's words the week before, specifically how he had managed to turn his life around a decade earlier after having found himself and his wife at the brink of a disaster. I needed a plan. I needed to reengineer my life so that my fundamental spiritual needs would be met. I needed a process to regenerate my soul. I wrote this thought down in my agenda, and began to consider what such a process might look like.

As ninety minutes ticked by, I'd contemplated many aspects of my life but had recorded little. I knew that taking time to think about my needs and to consider how I could begin to live my life fulfilling those needs was crucial. But there were Catherine's needs as well to factor into the equation, and Kyle's. Contemplating those around me and their intimate connection to my own journey, I gained a new appreciation of the fragile balance that must always be preserved between ourselves and our world. I believed that a professional therapist could help Catherine and me in establishing and maintaining this balance. I also felt that healing old wounds was a prerequisite to the change I was about to experience and consequently made a list of those with whom I needed to speak. Colleagues, neglected friends from the past, family, names of each I scribbled on the page in front of me. I felt I owed it to them, as important people in my life, to be vulnerable in expressing my past failings and my continuing commitment to doing better.

After ruminating a while longer, I headed for home. That evening after dinner I sat down with Catherine and Kyle and, in words that could be appreciated by a twelve-year-old, I began taking tiny steps towards reconciliation with my loved ones.

"You see, Kyle, what I'm trying to tell you is that I feel as if there's been something missing from my life," I explained. "And it's not anything that anyone can go out and buy or borrow from someone else. It's a feeling that you have inside."

"I don't get it, Dad," my puzzled son replied.

I continued, "I realize that since what I'm talking about can't be touched or seen it is difficult to grasp... but let me explain it this way. Think about how you felt when you worked so hard on your science project. All the research that you did at the library, the creativity you used, the hours you worked on building the model, all of this was an investment of yourself into something you dreamed of, a goal that you set for yourself, right? Now, think for a moment about how pleased you felt when you got an "A" for all your hard work. You felt pretty wonderful, didn't you?"

"Yeah, I always feel great when I get a good mark after working hard," Kyle added.

"But the feeling you had at that moment, it couldn't be touched or seen, it just was. It existed inside you, right?" I explained.

"I think I see what you mean," Kyle stated slowly.

"And how about the feeling you get when Mom hugs you before going to bed or when I hug you when I come home from a trip?" I offered.

Wide-eyed with renewed interest, Kyle jumped in, "I feel special. I feel good inside."

Then Catherine helped me explain, "And Kyle, when we go to church sometimes and speak with God or when we say prayers before going to sleep, remember what you said to me about how that makes you feel?"

With innocent comprehension, he shared his deepest thoughts, "I feel warm inside like everything is going to be OK, no matter how bad it seems. I feel excited about the things we are going to do together. I guess it makes me happy inside, so it's easy to be happy outside."

Listening to him speak, I realized that Kyle, probably like most children, was in touch with his soul. It takes a loss of innocence to compromise those things that we value. In any event, Kyle eventually seemed to understand that I had felt disconnected for a long time from the feelings he had described and that both Catherine and I wanted to become reacquainted with those feelings. He even asked how he could help us, to which we both responded that he could just continue being the wonderful person that he had become.

The next day at work would have been more unbearable if not for the pleasant recollections of the night before that helped me to deflect many of the icy stares that were directed at me. When I arrived in my office Jackie appeared agitated, so together we sat and shared a morning coffee. It was obvious that the door to our offices had been opened at some point in the night and that several filing cabinets had been rifled through. I'd insisted that Jackie leave all the cabinets unlocked and a complete set of the investigation papers contained within. Needless to say, the file had been removed. Smiling, I explained that this was to be expected and that we need not be concerned with further intrusions. She now understood the apparent contradiction in logic of the instructions I'd given her the previous morning and found herself able to surrender a knowing smile to me before returning to her desk.

My day at Medicon was comprised largely of visits to staff members both within my department and at sites scattered throughout the building. I chose this method to communicate to those closest to me what had happened during the executive meeting, as opposed to holding an assembly of staff members. In hindsight, that was a wise idea for a large gathering would have drawn unneeded attention. Besides, I wished to share some of my personal revelations with specific staff members as well. I made certain that I could meet with Paul and Karen together to inform them of the previous day's executive meeting, to ensure they were able to get copies of their files out of the building and to apologize to them for my previous insecurities. Forgiveness was given readily, and I began to find peace within.

Staff meetings weren't my only preoccupation that day. There were a dozen voice-mail messages from other executives who, out of some sort of perverted sense of collegiality thought they should phone to extort from me my 'true motivation' for what I had done or to offer 'anonymous commendation'. One executive's reason for calling was to offer me the name of a good psychologist! Not surprisingly, Tod Slater, who was the key focus of the investigation, was extremely angry with me and made that fact known in my voice mailbox. He had contained himself during the meeting and presentation, refusing even to make eye contact with me. Today, his usual volatility was unleashed, though like Harold Stoner, his assault was only verbal in nature with several messages comprised entirely of profanities directed at me. At some point during the day, Jackie brought a box into my office that had been received by courier from Biocodon. It was from Nathan. The parcel, which he had alluded to in his fax earlier in the week, had arrived. I anxiously opened it to find a note and a few books. I began reading,

My dear friend,

I've been thinking of you this past week and reflecting on the discussions we have shared. I do hope you are managing well on this new path you have chosen to follow. Your challenges have reminded me of the anxiety that I too experienced in the early days of my own spiritual rebirth. To help you to cope and get you off on the right foot, I am enclosing a few of my favourite books. They provided me direction and comfort during a period in my life when I felt my internal compass was incapacitated. I hope they prove helpful to you as well. I've also enclosed a personal journal within which you can capture your emotions, your struggles, and your victories. Be good to yourself and to those you love. Freedom and peace lie within you.

Yours truly,
Nathan

The book titles were eclectic with themes ranging from spiritual discovery to achieving wholeness and love. I remember feeling excited to discover their contents when I packed them into my briefcase. It was nearly six o'clock by the time I retreated from the office and I suspected one of the latest nights I'd find myself there for some time.

After an effortless Friday, Catherine and I committed to each other to spend quality time together over the weekend doing things we hadn't done for years. With Kyle spending Saturday afternoon and night with a hockey friend, we decided to take a drive out of town. We hiked and laughed and found a romantic spot within a forested park to enjoy a late picnic lunch and although the temperature was not conducive to our desires, we found our passion for each other was enough to keep us warm as we made love amongst the spruce and pines. Later, we drove around aimlessly, stopping when something caught our fancy and, although intent to return to Deerborne that evening, decided against it when we found quaint accommodation in a wonderful little bed and breakfast inn. Strolling the grounds of the inn that evening along a maze of well-lit gravel paths, we talked about our spiritual quest and our dreams for life.

Catherine began the conversation, "I know I've said this to you already, but I'm very proud of you, Ian. Few people would do what you have done in defense of their principles."

"Thanks, sweetheart. I only wish I'd done it a lot sooner. The fact is I wouldn't have even recognized the problem or had the strength to do anything about it without the support of so many people. I don't think I'm the brave one. After all, we're fine financially. It's people like Karen and Paul who have the most to lose, yet they've put their necks on the chopping block willingly. Now, that's strength of character."

"Do you really think that their careers are in jeopardy?"

"If Stoner has his way, I'm sure the three of us will be canned."

Catherine continued with a concerned voice, "You're not worried for your own career are you?"

"No, I'm not. I'm sure that something will come along. I'm really thinking more about my staff than myself at this point. But, they're all good people. I doubt that they'll have much trouble finding new positions."

Catherine picked up on the trepidation in my voice, "Any regrets?" she queried.

"None. I wanna work within an organization that values me for who I am and what I stand for. I lost sight of myself, both at work and at home, and in the process allowed my relationships to suffer and turned my back on my values. I've neglected the friendship I used to feel with God and that's created a huge void in my life. I know that now, and I wanna change. If you're willing, I want to work with you to regenerate our souls."

"Despite all of the reading I've done and all the courses I've attended, nothing has prepared me for the kind of spiritual growth I've ached for more than those words," Catherine explained emotionally as the tears streamed from her eyes.

The days that followed were likewise filled with introspection and conversation, as we attended our first private session with the therapist Catherine's friend had referred to us. By Thursday, April 8, I'd been contacted by Medicon's Board of Directors to present the findings of the investigation at a special meeting to be held the following Tuesday. I felt a sense of relief that finally I'd be bringing this chapter of my life to a close so, at the day's end, I retraced the familiar drive to my favorite cafe to enjoy some peace. As I entered the place that had become a sort of spiritual sanctuary for me, I found my friend Karl seated in the far corner, able to observe the entire room. He noticed me and by way of his smile and a subtle hand gesture, invited me to sit with him. I bought a large cappuccino and, making my way to his table, smiled and said hello. Karl had apparently been sitting there for the better part of an hour at that point and, although he had to leave soon to pick up his granddaughter at the train station, he was keen to learn how I'd been doing the previous few weeks. I volunteered how I put my newly rediscovered spiritual freedom into practice the previous week during the executive meeting and how I continued to work on reacquainting my mind and body with my soul.

"I'm finding this process to be very nebulous," I began. "Since there's no map or blueprint to follow, I'm often feeling anxious. I've been trained to approach challenges in a systematic way, but when it comes to my own spirituality I'm having problems deciding where to begin."

Nodding his head in acknowledgment, Karl interjected, "So, your mind is filled with competing theories on how or where to start, right?"

"Yes, that's exactly it. Sometimes I sit for hours and think about everything. But there isn't any sense to it all, no pattern emerges. Instead, I feel overwhelmed, often like I'm about to have an anxiety attack. This can't be good for me," I suggested.

"You're right," Karl acknowledged, "It's not good for you to feel anxious, but you can overcome that. You see, you control your thoughts and your reactions to those thoughts, but you're still behaving like a man in desperation. In your mind, you run from door to door like a madman in search of something. Since you don't know what you're looking for, your level of anxiety increases as you acquire additional information at each doorway. Try this. Find a quiet place free of distractions. Take several deep breaths. Focus on your breathing. As you breathe in and fill your lungs to capacity, imagine your body being bathed in purity. Then, slowly exhale. And as you breathe out, picture the poisons in your soul being washed away from you. Do this several times, even if you feel lightheaded. Then begin to think about what brings you peace, what makes you happy. Think about Ian Archer as a child, an adolescent, a young adult, and as a successful businessman, and try to visualize yourself as a soulful being. This is your starting point. Soon you'll appreciate what you need to achieve wholeness and, with those definable goals, you can begin to work towards their fulfillment. Just remember, this takes time. You can't rush the process. Your spirit will keep tempo to the rhythm of your development and growth."

Skeptical, but respectful of Karl's experience, I submitted, "I'll try that, Karl, thank you."

"Let me know how it goes, my friend, but for now you'll have to excuse me. My granddaughter, Lisa, from Spokane, will be attending her freshman year at the University of Chicago in the fall. She's arriving here today for a visit to get familiarized with the city. And she's going to get her grandpa to give her the tour," Karl said with obvious pride.

"You must be proud. I hope you have a wonderful visit and thank-you for your words of encouragement. They mean a lot to me," I said while I shook his hand goodbye.

"Not at all, Ian. Oh, and by the way, here's my number if you'd like to chat sometime. I still keep an office at the college and my home number's on the back. Don't hesitate to use either," Karl offered as he slipped a business card in my hand.

"Thanks, I'll do that." I'd hoped that some day he would offer me his number for I'd wanted on several occasions in the past to reach him, but didn't want him to feel on the spot if I'd asked. In hindsight, I suppose my own neuroses had impaired my judgment of the man and his potential reaction.

I nursed my beverage for another hour thinking about Karl's words, reflecting on Nathan's suggestions as well as those of the therapist Catherine and I had seen for the first time a few days before. I spent several minutes just 'being' in this space. I listened to the soft music, felt the comfort of the surroundings, and closed my eyes to allow myself to experience peace. It was a combination of emotions that led my spirit at that moment to christen this place. To me, this was a real sanctuary, it was the place where I could retreat from the artifice of life and just be me, where I could think and be creative, both in mind and spirit. It had become a haven from the storms that rocked my world. It was a magical place that only really became known to me when I allowed myself the freedom to heal. For me, this place was not just a café; it was The Soul Café.

Following Karl's instructions, I spent several hours meditating over the weekend. The backyard was a handy retreat, but I also found success walking through a nearby park. I sharpened my senses to observe the most subtle details in the veining of the leaves of a plant or the colors splashed across the forest floor, or the way the sun cascaded through the canopy of the trees. I wrote in the journal that Nathan had given me to capture my feelings and to pose the inevitable questions for which I had no immediate answers. During this time my thoughts focused around those things that fed my spirit.

I felt very much at peace.

By Monday morning, I could feel a difference in my physical being as if I were infused with energy and devoid of anxiety. Perhaps Karl was right, I thought. That evening Catherine and I visited the therapist again and we shared our respective experiences. Catherine suggested that she would like to try a spiritual retreat with me and, despite my immediate willingness to do so, we were advised against it at this early stage in our 'rebirth' as our therapist called it. Nonetheless, we left that session feeling as if we were beginning a new life together and we were excited at our prognosis. When we arrived home and said goodnight to Kyle, I felt an emotional charge course through me. I felt compelled to capture my feelings in writing, so with my wife's encouragement, I retreated to the living room and began to put down the ideas in my journal. For the first time in fifteen years my words spilled on to the page as a poem. I wrote for hours, taking a long pause between each verse to try to accurately convey my thoughts. As if seeking a reminder of my first few steps out of the darkness into the light, my soul guided my heart and my hand, foretelling a promise of hope and happiness.

Spiritual Regeneration

There comes a time in your life
when the simple act of living
floods your mind with questions.
Your soul starves for purpose.
You feel anemic, wasted, incomplete.
Like a diet of black and white
that hungers for the passion of red,
or the serenity of green, or the peace of blue,
You've known this hunger for far too long.

You find yourself gasping for air,
struggling to remember how to breathe.
You seek answers encrypted in the pages of your journal.
You seek answers in the keepsakes of your mind,
for so long lost and forgotten.
Your complacency to live in the security of banal emptiness
is drowned by a terrific flood of memories and emotions.
You are overwhelmed.

And all that you hear,
and all that you see,
and all that you do,
conspires to build a future,
out of hollow promises and broken spirit.

Like an orphaned child,
bereft of guidance,
every turn is an unfamiliar journey.
Every step taken is one in fear.

Until that moment,
when a voice speaks to you
through the chaos.
And you're no longer afraid,
And you understand your hunger,
And you understand your passions
are as necessary to you as air,
and need to be fed.
And you are wrapped in the comfort of sheer joy,
and you are free.

And the voice that spoke to you,
that awoke your spirit,
that challenged you for more...
that was your own voice.
You set your spirit free to seek a new way of being,
a better way,
where peace envelops you
and the energy of all living forces
gives you strength and hope and joy.
And you make a covenant with yourself
that you want to be whole,
that you need spiritual love,
and that you are worthy of happiness.

And the years of subsistence and avoidance,
that have been your bread and water could return

because this diet is familiar to you,
and because new liberty can be frightening.

But you are tired of compromise,
and hungry for fulfillment,
and you are strengthened
by the energy of a reaffirming soul.
And so you release your spirit to honor,
and to celebrate
the endless possibilities of freedom and love.

Meditation on the Run

> *Be the change you want to see in the world.*
>
> Mohandas Gandhi

Tuesday, April 13th, I found myself reflecting deeply on my career at Medicon and what my impending meeting with the Board of Directors might mean for my future. I had been asked to present at 1:30 p.m. at the Chicago Hilton, the usual location for the Board's monthly meeting. Having rehearsed my presentation countless times, I decided I was ready and, seeking a distraction from the task that lay ahead of me, I opted to go into the office for a few hours. The polarized feelings amongst head office staff

towards my presence were obvious when I entered the building. There were many that, due to their allegiance to the pow-
erful sales machine in the company, treated me as a leper.
Then there were those who had worked with me in the past.
Perhaps they felt their futures within the firm were precarious
due to Stoner's threats of layoffs and hence had little to lose
through their public encouragement of me. I preferred to
think, however, that this group of people knew my character
from having worked with me over the years and celebrated
the fact that finally an executive was prepared to challenge
the status quo within the firm. Regardless, I was empathetic
to everyone, for they each had their own stuff to deal with.
Besides, I could go crazy if I chose to second-guess every reaction. I remember thinking, though, that Karl would have
found these eclectic human behaviors fascinating.

When I reached my office Jackie was surprised to see me
especially in light of the significance of the impending meeting, but after I explained my need to be distracted, she
seemed to understand. It was then I learned that Harold
Stoner would be attending the meeting as well. It was cus-
tomary in most organizations for the chief executive and one
or two other key executives also to maintain seats on the
company's Board. In fact, it was not unusual for the CEO to
concurrently hold the position of Board chairperson as well.
Fortunately for Medicon, Stoner did not assume that role.
Despite that, he did sit on the Board and routinely attended
their meetings. I presumed, however, that the Board would
have perceived this matter to be somewhat removed from
the ordinary and would have asked for Stoner's absence until
the issue was resolved. Although initially rattled, I composed
myself and it wasn't long before Jackie and I were enjoying
a good therapeutic laugh over the whole situation.

I spent an hour or so engaged in mindless administrative tasks, then broke from the monotony to see Paul and Karen one final time before the Board meeting. I wanted to be absolutely confident of the details of the investigation; I wanted to capture every thought that each beleaguered employee had surrendered, convey every emotion that was felt. When I was satisfied that I'd regained the sickly impression of moral poverty that the firm had so insidiously instilled over the years, I headed downtown to share my testimony. I remember being spiritually divided, with memories of the past competing with my regenerated self as I navigated my way to the Hilton. But rationalization of the past with the present proved to be the cord of credibility that wove its way throughout my monologue that afternoon. The Board really seemed to feel my anger, my sorrow, my fear and at one point, as my emotions peaked, they experienced the pain of my once-abandoned soul. In hindsight, I wished that Stoner had witnessed all my feelings, but the Board had asked him to leave prior to my arrival. My presentation gripped each of those in the room. When I'd finished and provided the necessary evidence from the files, I was thanked profusely. Ms. Fairbanks, who'd volunteered little emotion during the meeting, rose and escorted me out of the room and down to the mezzanine of the hotel.

"You know, Mr. Archer, what you've done is a brave thing," she began.

"How so?" I asked, wondering what exactly she meant by 'brave'.

She continued, "In my experience, few executives are prepared to compromise their positions or job security by speaking out against their own organization."

"Well," I suggested, "I felt that I couldn't continue to blindly condone these improprieties. In my opinion, the future of Medicon is on the line. Either we accept the environment that we have created and the consequences to the firm's operations down the road, or we take a stand and try to repair things before it's too late."

"And you've done just that, with passion and eloquence. I might add the Board is extremely grateful to you and promises its actions will be swift and just," Valerie said sternly.

"Thank you for your kind words." I said. "I'm so pleased you agreed to stay at that executive meeting a few weeks ago. Without your presence, I doubt that we would've gotten this far so soon."

In response to my words, Valerie Fairbanks lowered her voice to a whisper, "Ian, if the truth be known, the Board has been concerned with Harold Stoner's leadership for some time, and felt that we needed to witness a few executive meetings to determine whether our suspicions were true. Obviously, they were."

Exchanging handshakes, we said our good-byes. That afternoon I left the undisciplined fervor of downtown Chicago where, like children anxious to play, the city's workers had been dismissed into already clogged streets and had begun to claw their way home.

After calling Jackie from my car to report briefly on the meeting and hopefully reassure her, I decided to take advantage of the late afternoon sun and stretched my legs in one of Deerborne's many parks. As I walked along a mossy trail in the warmth of the April sun, the scenery looked like something out of a Robert Frost poem and I paused to soak up its serenity. I could hear squirrels darting across the forest floor and birds teasing one another with song. I found the trunk of a lightning-struck pine tree laying next to the path, so I stopped to sit on it and absorb my surroundings. The air was filled with the smell of cedar and moss. This was complemented by the lingering scent of the fallen pine tree upon which I was perched and upon which Mother Nature had only recently released her fury. The bouquet was sublime. I closed my eyes and breathed deeply, thinking only about the peace of the moment and how it so beautifully filled my soul and brought joy to my heart. Each time I inhaled I envisioned every recess of my body being satisfied with the essence of happiness. And with every exhalation, I released the hostility of an embittered world that had reluctantly forfeited its claim over me. I knew this place for less than an hour, but I had known it since my life began and I was now sure that it would remain a part of me forever.

My afternoon meditation in the park was deliciously therapeutic, I explained to Catherine that evening when I arrived home. She had left work early, around 3:00 p.m. to be home for Kyle and me and to prepare dinner. Catherine was anxious to learn how the meeting had gone, so I quickly summarized it for her. She also wanted to offer me praise for the poem I'd written the night before and had left for her to review in the morning. Later, she told me that it moved her deeply. I was pleased, and explained that I'd written those words to release the emotions that had been caged inside me for so long. I was trying, as Nathan had described to me weeks before, to impress myself. With that poem, I felt as if I'd been successful and felt that I'd begun to heal at last. Catherine, too, in her own way was each day busily engaged in meditative practices. Usually, these were considerably different from my own, but they proved to be very effective for her. As the weeks went by, we each read, meditated, and were guided by the help of our therapist. And due to our renewed commitment to one another and to those around us, we made the time to talk about our dreams and goals. I told Catherine I wished to get in better physical shape to complement my new spiritual physique. We developed a schedule for us all to visit the local community center which provided ample opportunities to atone for the physical failings of our past. In actual fact, though, Catherine and Kyle had always been active and my wife, albeit seven years younger than myself, was in excellent physical condition. Such was not the case with me and so I began a regimen of toning and cardiovascular exercise. I decided to try running but felt somewhat bored on an indoor treadmill, so I scouted out a neighborhood trail and became one of those local runners I'd previously scowled at jealously. Actually, to describe myself as a runner would be overstating my abilities, for at times the image was not particularly attractive and my pace in general was closer to that of jogging. In any event, I found my new exercise program helped me both become more respectful of my body and protected and preserved my mental agility by managing the stress in my life.

And stress management proved to be a valuable asset in the weeks that followed the Medicon Board meeting of April 13th. Within days of the meeting, a notice arrived by messenger at my office. It was final formal approval by the Board to proceed with the Biocodon alliance. The Board had authorized me to endorse all of the necessary documents, preempting the usual processing by the President. With this information, I contacted Nathan Currie directly to share the good news. I took the opportunity to extend an invitation to him and his wife to travel to Chicago at Medicon's expense to officially close the deal and to celebrate by way of an intimate gathering of senior executives, Board members, and local dignitaries. Though seldom on official lists of invitees, often a few key financial reporters could be found at these gatherings to provide advance media attention to Medicon stock. All of these preparations were normal protocol for announcements of such import, but I was unusually anxious and excited for my visitor's arrival this time. Nathan and Helen would touch down at O'Hare on the morning of May 2nd. Until then, my staff would be occupied with organizing the event. Public Relations would generate news releases and press packages. Business Development staff would begin to meet with operational management at Biocodon to iron out any wrinkles in manufacturing, pricing, marketing and distribution, while the Government Affairs staff would begin to prepare submission packages for Medicare and Medicaid bureaucrats to review. The news was in every way positive and provided a much-needed infusion of excitement around which my team could once again come together.

My new-found autonomy on this project should have signaled to me what was about to occur, but I was still amazed at the expediency and decisiveness of the Board's actions with regard to the investigation.

In an unprecedented move, the Medicon Board terminated both Harold Stoner and Tod Slater's employment along with Slater's two directors. Later, I learned that to prevent them from speaking out against the firm, all but Slater received significant severance packages. The Board decided not to prosecute Slater for his actions in return for a written confession of his inappropriate behavior and forfeiture of any further rights or privileges from Medicon. Each of the other recommendations originally spelled out by Karen and

Paul was agreed to in its entirety. But perhaps most satisfying and surprising in the Board's announcements was the fact that a new chief executive had been recruited to return the firm to its former days when the human spirit was embraced and humanity was the first requirement of every employee. My old friend and mentor, Scott Ashbury, had returned. Though five years older, he appeared to be ten years younger due in part to a new therapy that controlled his hypertension better than ever and to a change in exercise and diet that saw him shed twenty unwanted pounds. He had been asked by the Board to return to Medicon's helm for a one-year period and, out of the love of a challenge and the love of a company he'd helped shape for thirty years, he accepted. Scott's welcoming announcement to the company took place in the auditorium with several Board representatives, including the Chair and Valerie Fairbanks, present. The dismissed employees had been escorted out of the building the day before, amidst a great deal of staff fervor. The rest of the executive behaved, for the most part, like a pack of rabid dogs. Some began to spread rumors about my own motivations behind the investigation, suggesting I was anxious to rise to the top of Medicon and would do anything to get there. 'Stepping on the backs of others' was a phrase found attached to my actions far too frequently. As a result of this, I was once again given occasion to question the sincerity of those coworkers who at times had called me friend. I tried to be philosophical about their actions, as Nathan had suggested, but found it difficult to hold my head high when colleagues were swinging their metaphorical axes. Then there were those who were crippled with fear for their jobs, most of whom had done nothing wrong, but had been accustomed to living a life of cowering to the loud obnoxious will of Stoner, Slater and others. Like a cat in a room full of rocking chairs, I felt very uneasy for the first few days that followed Scott's return. But, in his own way, Scott had made it clear to me that he hadn't lost his highly intuitive sense about people. On day one, he addressed the executive with energy and direction, hallmarks of a true leader. He clearly outlined sales performance targets, but he also shared his vision for the type of caring organization he wished to recreate. In addition, he highlighted several new human resource policies that he wanted developed to protect the staff against harassment and abuse. He announced the establishment of the position of ombudsman. An executive member reporting directly to him, the bearer of this title would assume responsibility for dealing with all of the injustices experienced by staff, beginning with those of the past several years. In Scott's words, "The success of all of our efforts over the next few years is dependent upon rectifying our failings of the past, for Medicon's future is forged out of experiences of its past. The weakest link in the chain defines the ultimate strength of the organization." Although the Human Resources department reacted negatively to these announcements, since they felt the issues fell within their own purview, it was obvious to everyone in the room that Stoner had rendered that department helpless and therefore not directly responsible for subsequent issues arising out of harassment. Furthermore, Tod Slater and Harold Stoner had so effectively camouflaged the rampant abuses, that Human Resources had had no inkling of their occurrence.

Scott Ashbury would change all of that. He was an enlightened executive who, during his ascension through the ranks of management, always put the needs of his staff first. He demonstrated his respect for each individual and for their contributions, as people, not simply as drones fulfilling their duties, but for all of their life experiences that could benefit their fellow workers. The anecdotes I heard from Scott proved this. Administrative staff had provided invaluable leadership advice as a consequence of their experiences coaching their kids' baseball teams. Maintenance crews, who distinguished themselves in their local Rotary Clubs, had provided valuable contacts to the company. And management trainees, whose experience volunteering on a community board, helped resolve difficult team conflicts in the office. Scott impressed upon me years before the value of every individual and the diversity of their experiences and the importance of acknowledging and celebrating this resource pool. As president, he had implemented a company-wide program to encourage employees to volunteer in their communities, providing five days per employee per year of paid leave for this purpose. He also liberated staff from the rigidity of a nine to five work day through the provision of flex time. An on-site fitness center, wellness programs for disease prevention, a subsidized day-care cooperative, and a generous benefits program were further examples of the man's commitment to attracting and retaining staff. Scott had seen the impact that these and other initiatives had on productivity, worker satisfaction, absenteeism, turnover and, ultimately, the balance sheet. The bottom line was that respect for and acknowledgement of the individual clearly brought about positive financial benefits to Medicon. As Scott put it, "It's the right thing to do, and it feels good doing it!" Such had been Scott Ashbury's legacy, but it was sadly short-lived, for systematically many of his initiatives were whittled away at the hands of Harold Stoner who failed to appreciate their appeal and value. With Scott back at the helm, Medicon would surely experience a renaissance of thought and a heightened commitment to its people.

Following his remarks to the executive, Scott asked me to join him for a coffee in the cafeteria. Another noteworthy characteristic of the man was his desire to be seen by staff and to be accessible rather than hidden away in an imposing office that shouted out condescension to all who dared to enter. As we filled our cups and proceeded to the cashier, several staff who had known the man years earlier, heartily welcomed him back. We sat down and Scott immediately began, "You know, Ian, though I never thought in my wildest dreams that it would happen, I'm nonetheless very glad to be back. I believe that even the missus is pleased. She was growing tired of seeing my face around all day, anyway."

"It's great to have you back, Scott," I replied in earnest. "The place has definitely not been the same since you left."

My old mentor went on, "Well, that's what we're here to fix. I've read your report and the investigative notes and, as I mentioned to the troops earlier, I'm committed to repairing the damage of the past and to building for the future. Before I start that, though, I wanted to speak with you personally. Specifically, in your opinion, what happened here when I left five years ago? I mean, how did the executive behave when Stoner was elected president? And how quickly did you notice changes in the way that others were being treated?"

I began to recount, as best I could, the events of the past five years. I felt embarrassment for my career ascension during this time and for my denial of, or disregard for, behaviors that were shameful. I knew I could rationalize away my guilt, but the fact remained that as an officer of the company, my responsibility to exemplify and uphold ethical behavior extended throughout the firm. Departmental boundaries or organizational charts, though convenient scapegoats, do not confer immunity on any of us from protecting basic human respect and dignity.

Scott sensed my guilt and shame and understood. "I want you to know, Ian, that you earned your promotion four years ago. In fact, it was discussed while I was still running the show here. And your avoidance of conflict early on in your tenure as Vice President is understandable. The fact is that it was you who finally recognized the issue and it was you who was prepared to risk everything to make reparations."

I corrected my friend, "Not everything—I wasn't prepared to compromise myself. No matter what the consequence, I refuse to live a lie again."

"Of course not, nor should you," Scott concluded. "But tell me, I'm curious to know what happened to awaken those feelings within you that drove you to expose the problems and those responsible. After all, you tolerated them for four years. Why the crusade now?"

"I'm sure that's a question many have on their minds right now, especially Harold Stoner and Todd Slater," I began. Then I continued on to explain the past several months of reflection, reading, discussion and therapy. Scott and I had always shared a healthy respect for each other and I considered him a friend, so it didn't feel odd to describe my quest for a more spiritually fulfilling life to him.

"What do you mean when you say you seek a spiritually fulfilling life? Are you referring to going to church more often? Or taking bible study classes or something like that?" he asked.

I was a bit surprised by his question. Not that I hadn't found myself answering it for others, but because I felt that

Scott was well-grounded spiritually. In hindsight, I now understand that he was simply assessing whether I knew what I was looking for out of life.

I offered him this: "Although what you describe may be the answer for some people, that's not what I mean. Spirituality to me is defining one's values and deep fundamental needs and nurturing them in everyday life. It's not just a question of finding time for your soul, but integrating sustenance for your soul into your life and celebrating its presence daily. And it applies to one's work life as well. We need to find love and trust and respect in our employment. Too frequently, the corporate world has rewarded performance at any cost, oblivious to how the achievements have been made. These corporations don't realize that condoning lies or deceit or acts performed on the backs of others provides fertile ground for employee dissatisfaction, productivity decline, and turnover. I believe that the individual who finds wholeness for their soul through their work, their home, their beliefs and their values is the one who becomes the true catalyst for greatness in others."

My answer provoked a smile and an approving nod from the man across the table. Extending his large, aged hand Scott remarked, "I'm very proud of you, Ian. You've grown a great deal over the last several months. I'm comforted by your comments and your values and am hopeful that you will share your ideas to help us with Medicon's spiritual regeneration. Oh, and by the way, when are you going to pick up that box you sent over to the house?"

"I'll tend to the box tonight if that's all right with you, Scott, and I'd be pleased to help out in any other way possible," I suggested as I shared a knowing glance with him. It was to Scott that I'd instructed Jackie send a copy of the investigative records in a sealed box for safe keeping, with instructions not to disturb its contents. Trust had always been a cornerstone of Scott's leadership, and I'd known that I could count on him to honor his word.

"Great," he began in response to my offer. "So Ian, what do you think of Paul? I've been reviewing his file and see he's been here at Medicon for some time, most of which has been working with you. His performance on this latest investigation has been exemplary, and I'd like to consider him for the new post of internal ombudsman. That is, if you don't object."

As I'd remembered, the man in front of me was a quick and precise observer of people and, to his credit, wanted to demonstrate decisive action and send a clear message throughout the firm that changes were going to happen right away.

"An excellent choice," I replied without hesitation.

After two hours of discussion with the man, I already felt an incredible tide of hope wash over the firm. Though there was much to be done, the man who could do it had returned.

The days that preceded Nathan and Helen's visit are a bit of a blur to me now. There was a flurry of activity occurring within Medicon, in preparation for Biocodon's visit and in the implementation of new policies, as well as in the normal sales and marketing functions. Punctuating the hectic pace over the course of those weeks were periodic breaks at home to allow Catherine and me time to meditate. Sometimes we would go outside to the backyard before breakfast to breathe in the intoxicating freshness of a spring morning. With dew bathing our feet we would tread to the edge of the lawn where the tall conifers stood sentinel-like. When we'd soaked up enough of the babbling brook, or the play of squirrels, we retreated back to the house, following the path our feet had made in the grass moments before. On other occasions, when the chill outside dissuaded us, we'd find peace for our souls indoors. We would sit cross-legged and back-to-back on the plush living room carpet, while the power of our touching bodies carried us into a state of sublime tranquility. Our physical proximity seemed to comfort us sufficiently and enable us to achieve our own individual state of bliss. I felt our souls were entwined giving us the individual strength to achieve happiness. Our spirits were learning to dance. In those all too brief moments, Catherine and I experienced a heightened sense of spiritual love and wholeness.

But opportunities for meditation were not the only escapes we engineered for ourselves. There was our new fitness routine in which the whole family participated. I found running to be very therapeutic both physically and spiritually, as when I focused on breathing rhythmically it tended to purge other thoughts from my head. As time progressed and my metabolism improved, breathing in and out took on a mantra-like quality that I personally found very peaceful. My mind was becoming clear and able to acknowledge my spiritual needs, a critical step to ensuring sustained support for the soul amidst a world of competing agendas. And, of course, Catherine and I continued to seek professional help to open up to one another, to manage our fears, and to allow ourselves to be vulnerable with each other. We were waging a war against apathy and spiritual malaise, with the battleground being our hearts and souls and minds.

It had been three weeks since returning from my trip with Nathan and nearly as long since Catherine and I began our process of regeneration, when we agreed that we could all use a break. So with my father soon to be returning from his cruise, we planned a week of vacation to visit him in mid-May. But, first, there would be my much-anticipated visitor from Oxford and the official ceremony to announce the Medicon-Biocodon alliance.

On Sunday, May 2nd, Catherine accompanied me to the airport to greet Helen and Nathan Currie. Kyle was deeply engrossed in baseball at this time and so his day had been planned in advance at a baseball camp. He wouldn't be home until 5:00 p.m. After finding our guests, we took them to their hotel situated near Medicon and offered to escort them around Chicago that afternoon. Dinner was to be in our home at 6:30 p.m. They graciously accepted our invitation, enabling us all to get to know each other better. I thanked Nathan for the books he'd sent and, aware that Helen had been apprised of the subject of Nathan's and my discussions while on our Biocodon trip, I openly discussed what had transpired for Catherine and myself since. They both seemed pleased and genuinely interested in our personal journey and shared many of their own experiences with us. Just as it had been with Nathan and me, the discussion between the four of us was uncannily comfortable and easy. It was evident that there was a feeling of peace amongst us as we enjoyed afternoon tea at 4:00 p.m. back at our home. The peace was short-lived, however, as Kyle announced his arrival shortly thereafter and eagerly entertained us with his dramatic recollections of the day's events. Kyle continued to shine in the spotlight throughout dinner, but began to tire by nine. By ten he was fast asleep. Our guests had likewise shown signs of fatigue and when I offered to return them to their hotel, there was no opposition. It was a wonderful beginning to what was to be a highly memorable visit.

The following day I had breakfast with Nathan at his hotel, after which we went together to the corporate offices of Medicon. Helen had promised herself some pampering at the hotel spa and therefore was quite happy on her own. Although a guest of the Medicon complex before, Nathan again remarked at the size of the place as we drove up and he seemed embarrassed by its opulence. Knowing the internal strength of the man, I suspected his blushed cheeks were for Medicon rather than for Biocodon, for his needs were simple and his commitment was to people not to bricks and mortar. Not that Biocodon's facilities were exactly austere, for a degree of comfort and design was important in this business to convey stability and success to potential investors and to provide a relaxing environment for staff. But Medicon's surroundings overindulged the eye as was the practice of the chief executive who approved its design, Harold Stoner. Regardless, Nathan and I settled into my office where I provided the details of the latest changes in management. My friend was not surprised to hear of the tumult that had been witnessed within these walls only a few weeks earlier, but was empathetic to the situation I'd endured at the time.

"Now I can better understand the struggles you faced during our travels, my friend," Nathan offered in an almost apologetic tone. "You were obviously torn between loyalty and principle."

"I hadn't really considered my struggle in that light before," I replied as I continued to reflect on Nathan's assessment. "Certainly, my principles weighed heavily in my ultimate decision, but I'm not convinced that loyalty was at issue here."

In his usual polite manner, Nathan countered with, "Perhaps not. But from your remarks during our travels I suspected that you felt an internal conflict emerge around your loyalty to your fellow executive, to your divisional staff who faced imminent layoffs, to your family, and to yourself. Forgive me if I interpreted the situation incorrectly. I don't mean to presume...."

"Not at all, Nathan," I interjected, "there's nothing to forgive. In fact, you're quite right. My internal struggles for weeks had involved the impact of my decision on each of those mentioned, but as I learned from our discussions, the first step to achieving wholeness is truthfulness. Being true to myself and my needs enabled me to acknowledge that there was only one action to take and, by realizing that truth, I was serving all of the other constituents' best interests as well. I guess what I'm trying to say is that once I recognized the need to be true to myself in making my decision, my soul knew peace."

"Without sounding condescending, I'd like to tell you that I am proud of you, Ian. You've experienced tremendous spiritual growth as a result of this process."

Following our discussion, I introduced Nathan to Scott Ashbury and to several other executives who'd be in attendance the following evening at the formal alliance announcement. I also took the opportunity for Nathan to meet with all of my staff at a private luncheon I'd arranged. After all, I reasoned, it would be the operational staff who'd make the alliance a success and it was their collective efforts that had made the announcement possible. The luncheon was very well received with staff lingering behind to speak with Nathan until shortly before 3:00 p.m. I would've encouraged it to continue had it not been for the signs of fatigue displayed by my guest. After pausing en route to my office for a 'biological break', we returned to collect our briefcases. There was still one stop I wished to make with

Nathan before returning him to his hotel, so we bid Jackie goodnight and proceeded to the car.

"The Soul Cafe" was alive and well, as the sound of a double bass sculpting a sultry pulse could be heard as we approached the front door. A few patrons occupied the room, but finding a comfortable seat was effortless, so with large foamy mugs of cappuccino in tow we made our way to two inviting chairs and sat down.

"Welcome to the Soul Café, Nathan. I found this place several months ago and unlike any other coffee shop or bistro I've visited, it soothes my spirit's daily aches and pains. I've done some of my best thinking here, so much so that it's become like a second office to me," I stated proudly.

"I can understand that," Nathan began in response as he more closely examined our surroundings. "The colors are soothing, the music pleasing, and the aromas are wonderfully tempting. It's a true sensory experience. Even the chairs evoke comfort the way the cushions wrap around the body. It's almost as if we're being cuddled in the arms of a loved one. I'm not surprised you find yourself able to think more clearly and be more productive in your work in such an environment."

As Nathan spoke, I listened, and suddenly was struck with an idea that I needed to take to Scott. I took out my agenda and instructed myself to arrange a meeting with him as soon as possible.

"Forgive me, Nathan, I don't mean to be rude," I apologized, "but an idea just came to me that I need to note; otherwise it'll be lost."

With his self-deprecating humor, Nathan trivialized the incident and began to recount instances when he, the absent-minded professor, as Helen would say, would write entire manuscripts during dinner so as not to lose his train of thought. And so, our afternoon carried on, two friends blessed with the capacity to recognize happiness and to honor it in their lives.

Despite the rigor of the itinerary planned for Nathan and his wife, Catherine and I managed to share several hours of peaceful time with the Curries during their visit. Their friendship was especially welcomed by Catherine who, for the first time in years, felt comfortable speaking with another woman about her own personal struggles. She later confirmed her feelings towards our new friends and told me that the opportunity to share a part of herself with others with complete trust was very therapeutic for her. This bond was no more apparent than during our farewells at the airport five days after their arrival. Although we knew our contact would be maintained, indeed we agreed to vacation in Greece together the following October, Catherine's eyes nonetheless betrayed her usual stoic self and she wept. Her emotions were a potpourri of happiness for new friends, hope for the future, and pain for repressed needs. Helen stood by her and when the tears had retreated, the four of us shared a group hug.

On the ride back home that Thursday night, Catherine shared her thoughts with me, "I'm sorry for being so emotional back at the airport, Ian. Helen and Nathan must think I'm a complete basket case."

"Not at all, darling. I think they were flattered by how comfortable you are with them, and by your expression of genuine emotion," I assured her.

"I feel that I created a great bond with Helen. We talked and talked, and she helped me to examine my parents through different eyes. She explained some cultural and generational influences that put my mom's behavior during my adolescent years in an entirely different light. I really think that I should've given mom the benefit of the doubt."

Later that evening, the Torres residence received an unexpected phone call from their daughter. She spoke with her father, now retired from practice, and then with her mother. Over the course of two hours or more, amidst a choir of tears, explanations, and apologies, my wife forgave and was forgiven. Twenty years of negative emotions that had stifled the best parts of Catherine's character were finally released. I remember holding her that night in bed and how she slept deeply wrapped in the warmth of my embrace.

May was a beautiful month in Chicago, both in terms of the weather and the forecast for change at Medicon. I was able to relinquish much of my authority over the management of the Biocodon alliance to my staff, but still found opportunities to speak with Nathan on a regular basis. Scott had asked me for ideas for positive change in the company, and I happily worked on a host of potential initiatives I believed could help to recreate an environment of trust, recognition, and community. I proposed that the company consider several trust-building programs offered by outside consultants I'd been exposed to over the course of my career. Many of these were based around experiential learning opportunities, such as rock climbing or navigating deep in the woods while blindfolded. I suggested motivational speakers, recognition and reward programs, and the repatriation of benefits that Scott had implemented but which had later been lost. I added that quarterly town-hall meetings led by Scott would help the employees understand the corporate direction better and that a policy of open-door access for all employees to any manager or executive would help to disseminate ideas and issues more rapidly and productively. Employees had to once again feel valued members of a team whose input was welcomed. Trust had to be restored. Finally, prompted by the notes I'd taken during my conversations with Nathan the previous week, I suggested to Scott that the company retrofit a part of the building's main floor to establish its own Soul Café. I proposed that the qualities that made the space so inviting to me and conducive to clearing the mind and releasing the spirit would be completely consistent with the needs of a beleaguered staff. Further, I added that the motivational presentations, staff development courses, or wellness seminars that would be offered could be part of the mandate of the Soul Café. This would not simply be a place for coffee, but rather a catalyst for changing behavior. We would create a haven for regenerating and expanding the soul. Executive and management instruction, stress management, leadership skills, team and trust building experiences, meditation, mentoring, and development of Medicon's corporate community could each be elements of its design. The Soul Café could be the unifying force that ensured a common direction and coordination to all of the company's staff development activities so as to maximize their impact. Scott listened intently and with excitement about my Soul Café ideas, interrupting occasionally to offer his own input. He agreed with the concept, asked me to develop a budget, and to determine the location for the facility. His satisfaction was apparent. Soon, my ideas would find a home in the hearts of Medicon's staff.

But before construction would start, Catherine, Kyle and I departed for a week-long visit with my father at the family homestead in upstate New York. After our plane touched down in Albany, we faced a ninety-minute drive west and arrived shortly after supper. My father, though seventy-four years of age, was in great health carrying himself as though he were a decade or so younger. After unpacking the rental car and fixing a quick bite to eat, Kyle went upstairs to play with his hand-held video game and, at the insistence of Catherine, I went for a walk with my father. The years had aged him in a dignified way. He retained his crop of silvery white hair, his gait, though perhaps a little slower, was not otherwise impaired, and he walked erect, never slouching. We talked about his recent trip and his voice was animated with the delight he'd found in the fellowship of many new friends. In particular, he spoke glowingly of a woman, a widowed school teacher, who'd offered him companionship and made him laugh. I could tell he was apprehensive in describing her to me because of his uncertainty as to how I would react. It had been almost four years since my mother's passing and, though I knew no one could replace her either in my mind or in his, I also knew my father was very lonely. For the first time since she died, I put his feelings before my own. I suppose that up until then my own guilt and despair had blinded me to my father's pain. In any event, I was pleased to learn that Steven Archer had found joy in his life and I told him so.

The week flew by as I renewed old acquaintances and proudly showed off my family to Dad's friends and neighbors, many of whom had descended upon the homestead in advance of our arrival to help prepare the house and to offer samples of their home cooking. Kyle loved the open spaces and the attention his grandfather paid to him. Catherine felt great peace in the house and would stroll the country lanes and meadows for hours, sometimes accompanied by myself or a neighbor, sometimes alone. As our departure loomed, I found opportunities to share my recent experiences with my Dad. On one such occasion we found ourselves perched on the top step of the covered porch at the front of the house. I'd always been impressed by the meticulous detail that craftsmen a century before had displayed in fabricating the gingerbread trim and the railings and the cornices that decorated the porch. My father showed his pride in the house by conscientiously preserving the original condition of each of these details. While sitting there, carried away in conversation on any number of topics, I happened to pose to my father the ageless philosophical question, "What's the meaning of life?"

Removing his hat and wiping his brow, he spoke with the wisdom of a lifetime of experience, "Son, I'm no expert but I think the answer to that question is as simple as this— it's finding happiness in your life. Now, I know that that means different things to different people, but as far as I can tell, true happiness is the essence of Life, and for forty-five years, your mother and I felt true happiness."

I remember sharing that moment with Catherine two days later as our plane soared westward, filtering out clouds as it ascended into perfect blue. She responded with a smile, a kiss, and a few words..." Your father's a wise man."

9

Surrendering to Our Spirtuality

> *And now here is my secret, a very simple secret:*
> *It is only with the heart that one can see rightly;*
> *what is essential is invisible to the eye.*
>
> Antoine de Saint-Exupery

S pending a week in the country with Dad turned out to be exactly what Catherine, Kyle and I needed to decompress. After all, we'd all felt considerable emotional tension over the previous six months or more and desperately needed a break. The time with my father also reminded Catherine that her own parents were long overdue a visit. It'd been five years since she'd last crossed their doorstep. And, then, primarily because we were vacationing in Orlando. At the time, the friction between Catherine and

189

her parents was obvious but, as I'd always done in the past, I kept Kyle out of earshot and ignored the rest. My wife had begun to heal many of those ancient wounds over the previous few weeks, and so I understood her interest in planning a trip to Miami shortly after our return from New York. In fact, around the same time, Catherine and I agreed that we also wanted to see my siblings, Marie and Shawn, and to visit with our old friends in California. It was sort of as if we were seeking atonement for our sins from those we had abandoned. We were trying to shed our past existence in favor of a new enlightened way of being. The fact is, though, that life's transitions from the ending of one phase to the beginning of the next are seldom so well defined. Often, our lives are riddled with ambiguity from dealing at times with the past while breaking new ground for our present. For Catherine and I, we bid farewell to our unfulfilled selves, as a new beginning was promising new hope.

And so as we returned to our work and to our routine in Chicago, endings were celebrated, beginnings were embraced, and we began to take back ownership of our lives. Realizing the importance of visiting with Catherine's parents, we sat down one evening with Kyle a few days after having returned from Dad's and, with a calendar in hand, we reserved the first available opportunity for a four-day weekend, June 4-7, and made the arrangements. With Kyle deeply immersed in studies and baseball, Catherine busy with a client's corporate restructuring, and me focused on my routine business and the newly approved Soul Café, the two weeks that followed swept by in no time.

Our reunion at the opulent Torres residence was expectedly emotional. The phone calls made in advance had released decades of repressed emotions. With an embittered past whittled away a teardrop at a time, Catherine eventually found forgiveness and understanding. She had come to realize that much of her anger towards her parents had surfaced in her mid-teens, as she challenged her father's beliefs and traditional attitudes towards women and was disappointed by her mother who had abandoned her daughter's defense. The naive ideals of an adolescent striving to prove both to her world and to herself that she was her own person and that she was worthy of respect, had been muted by the outdated undertones of traditional parents living in the culture of their ancestors.

The years and geography between Miles and Mary and their only child had allowed the myths of childhood to overshadow the realities. Ironically, although time and experience can endow us with wisdom and understanding, we often fail to apply that wisdom when we consider how events in our past occurred, what our role was in creating them, and how our history has influenced our present. Though painful for her, Catherine had come to find this truth during the months prior to our travels to Miami. She had acknowledged her past and, through contemplation and introspection, had accepted her responsibility in creating that past. It was largely due to Helen Currie's influence that Catherine came to trust her intuitive abilities. "In matters of greatest import to you, trust in your heart, not your head," Helen had suggested to her, during one of their afternoon strolls.

Catherine had known for a long time, of course, that if her past were preventing her from fulfilling her soul's needs for her future, she must invest time to resolve that past. That was completely reasonable logic, and yet for so long she had failed to take the necessary steps. I suspected her "rational self" had battled with her subconscious, for concealed within all of those years of reflection lay many, many fears. Some had probably foretold of continued parental abandonment, some of other types of disappointment, but all were real to my wife and at some level had tormented her for years. At least until Nathan and Helen's visit, when fate would provide Catherine with the strength and readiness to be vulnerable with someone who could help her. During the Curries' visit, Helen had instructed Catherine to live her truth by allowing herself to yield to her spiritual needs. "My dear," she had said in a wonderfully comforting voice, "Surrender to your spirituality. Trust in your heart and your soul will then know peace." Those words had been a catalyst for change in Catherine's life, as Nathan's had been for me in mine.

So, during our brief visit to Miami, Catherine spent hours and hours with her parents explaining herself to them. She acquired a new perspective on her Spanish heritage and came to understand and appreciate how it had permeated her parents' values. She asked difficult questions of both of them and, though she didn't always agree with their answers, found that she could better understand why they felt what they did. For the first time in twenty years, Catherine found respect for her parents. As they shared time together with each of us, Mary and Miles began to better appreciate the joys of their grandchild and how successful their daughter had been in her career and family. One warm evening after Kyle had gone to bed and the adults had retreated to the backyard patio to enjoy a glass of wine and each other's company, Catherine's parents told her how much pride and respect they had for her. Later, she explained to me as we prepared for bed that she couldn't remember any point in her life that she felt closer to them. She had a

spirited aura about her that evening that seemed to illumi-
nate our room. As I leaned over to kiss her goodnight, she
whispered in my ear with a playful grin and, happy to comply with her adolescent request, made love with her in her
parents' house.

The relatively mild temperatures Chicago had experienced throughout the spring were replaced by a colder
and very wet month of June. So it was when we returned
from our Florida weekend. In fact, the little brook that
usually trickled through our backyard had spilled over its
boundaries to create a large circular reservoir extending
beyond the tree line to the lawn. Coupled with the
famous Chicago winds coming off Lake Michigan, it was
the least hospitable June I could remember in our nine
years here. Despite the weather, Catherine, Kyle and I
kept busy, spending considerable time together as a family. We entertained ourselves playing games, watching
movies, reading and talking, all the while becoming closer and more respectful of each other's needs and differences. It was during one of these evenings I came up with
the notion of capturing our combined thoughts and values in both personal and family mission statements. I
can't remember exactly what led me to this idea, but it
was likely prompted by something I'd read in one of those
books Nathan had sent me. When I presented the concept
to our therapist during one of our visits, she responded
favorably and suggested that putting our most important
needs and values down on paper would immortalize
them. It would also allow each family member to provide
input and to articulate their own needs relative to the others', and to learn how each of us could contribute to the
others' fulfillment.

On our next available Saturday, shortly following our therapy session, Catherine and I decided to create our own missions. We thought we should begin by acknowledging the values that we held closest and most strongly. I suggested we think about the five people in our lives that we held in highest personal regard and for each of us to write seven to ten words that exemplified their values. After eliminating redundancies, over forty qualities remained when our two lists were combined. We then reviewed our notes and selected the ten values that we felt best described us as individuals. Distilling those ten attributes down to three was a more difficult challenge, but one we nevertheless managed. Catherine's were happiness, freedom, and nurturing, while mine were honesty, happiness, and integrity.

Once we got to this point, we paused to reflect on our accomplishments as I prepared a pot of Earl Grey tea. After our little break, we resumed by articulating the vision for our lives or, in other words, by defining our dreams, hopes and aspirations. During the visioning exercise we made sure we kept in mind the key values we'd identified earlier. Catherine then shared the product of her labor with me and I did the same. As I'd hoped and expected, our vision statements were remarkably similar. Essentially, we wished to contribute to the betterment of the world around us, helping ourselves and others to be liberated of pain, and to know happiness and peace. We envisioned a life of great personal joy and love where our individual growth would be celebrated together. For some time, we pondered our personal missions, the distillation of our values and goals and our vision for life. Our mission statements would have to reflect the people, activities, and events that, when properly unified, would animate our visions and bring them to life everyday. We thought quietly for several minutes on this subject before Catherine's face betrayed her emotions.

"What is it?" I asked hopefully.

Proudly, Catherine answered, "I think I understand what our mission is. At first I thought about it only for myself, but now I believe it's true for each of us."

"So, are you going to share it with me?" I inquired.

"It's exactly what Helen had said to me, that we need to surrender to our spirituality in all that we do. If we trust in ourselves and our faith, if we believe in our values and continually challenge ourselves to grow and to experience life, then we can achieve happiness for ourselves and for those whose lives we touch."

The more Catherine spoke, the more I believed she was right. Our mission had to be concise and had to be something for which actions could be taken every single day. With that in mind we drafted our first mission statement:

We will strive to be true to ourselves and to our values in our daily interaction with each other and the community around us.

Though simple in design, this statement captured the essence of our spirits and brought us great comfort. We'd already spent three hours arriving at this on a rainy Saturday afternoon, but our task was not complete until we could get Kyle involved in the process as well. So, the following afternoon we sat down with our son to do just that. But rather than have him think about creating a list of values on his own, we presented him with our forty-odd selections. We asked him to choose ten that best described himself. For several minutes he reviewed the page:

__ integrity	__ self-aware
__ accomplishes goals	__ empower
__ trustworthy	__ explorer
__ well-networked	__ contributor
__ honest	__ free
__ spiritual	__ volunteer
__ sincere	__ ambitious
__ seeks growth	__ pioneer
__ efficient	__ self-centered
__ proud of ancestry	__ inventive
__ collegial	__ social conscience
__ healthy	__ tolerant
__ diligent	__ protector
__ pursues happiness	__ genuine
__ flexible	__ nurturer
__ defender of rights	__ humane
__ confident	__ esteemed
__ financially wealthy	__ conformist
__ creative	__ aggressive
__ beautiful	__ tenacious
__ moral	__ environmentalist

After seeking clarification on a few, Kyle identified ten values for himself, which Catherine and I took great interest in. The exercise revealed qualities that we as parents had not perceived to be key to our son. He pronounced that he believed himself to be a "protector" and a "pioneer," two traits that had not occurred to Catherine or me. Nonetheless, once the ten had been noted, we created something of a game to help Kyle reduce his list down to three. We suggested that he pretend he was entering a large house with several rooms. At the end of a maze of seven interconnected rooms was a grand ballroom where a party was being held in his honor. All of his closest friends and family were already there awaiting his arrival, along with many people whom he'd never met before. There was music and lots of food and drink to enjoy and everyone awaited their host, especially those who'd never met him. They wanted to understand what Kyle was like. As he passed from room to room on his way to the ballroom, we told him he had to give up one quality on his list of ten. By the time he reached his destination, he was to enter with the three values he held to be most important. Those three values would define the core of his being to the whole room of awaiting guests. As expected, Kyle began this exercise quickly, but as he entered the fifth room, the choices became much more difficult for him. Finally, though, he entered the ballroom with "healthy," "protector," and "trustworthy" representing himself. Catherine and I were very proud of our son. We were moved, not by his selections, but by his honesty and trust in sharing his soul with us. We likewise revealed to Kyle our own final three values and spent some time describing why we felt what we did. For the rest of the exercise, we shared our reasoning with Kyle and invited him to contribute to our family's mission statement. He agreed with what we'd written and suggested we frame it and have it displayed in the house to serve as a reminder of our beliefs. It was a wonderful idea that added dignity and permanence to our weekend's work so we agreed to do just that. In celebration, we went out for dinner that evening feeling more aware of each other and more united in our understanding of the family's mission.

That period in my life was filled with many challenges, and I found myself frequently discussing my most profound thoughts with those I cared about deeply. Allowing ourselves to be vulnerable let Catherine and me explore the deepest, most private aspects of our lives. We began to trust in that inner force that guides each of us, relinquish control, and be open with our feelings. In hindsight, I believe this "leap of faith" was necessary in order for each of us to realize wholeness in our souls.

One particularly difficult issue that came to mind was how fully I could trust in and be truthful with Catherine. One evening as we lay on the sofa together, my head on her lap, we began talking about our pride in Kyle and his accomplishments. Just then, the thought of having another child entered my head. It had been five years since we'd entertained the subject and our lives had changed considerably since then, but I could still vividly recall the fighting that had ensued over this issue in the past. I didn't want to argue with Catherine, but I also knew we were different people with different values and needs from who we'd once been. So, I decided to be completely honest with her, for I knew that I had to embrace my mission and be true to myself. The fact was that I wanted to have another child, and so I posed the question to her.

"Catherine," I began, "as we've been speaking about Kyle, I've been thinking about conversations that we've had in the past. I was wondering whether you've given any thought to having another child?"

There was no response, which I took to mean that I'd caught her off guard. I continued, "Now, I know how you felt about it years ago, but I think we are different people now. We're not so caught up with the idea of keeping of up with everyone else. I feel as if we have so much to give and, although I know we'd have to make some significant changes in our lives, I'd very much like to have another baby with you."

"Ian, my silence doesn't mean I take objection to what you're saying, but rather is because of my surprise. You see honey, I've been late for about a week now, which has happened only once before in my life. I've been planning to take a home test for the last few days. I've also wanted to speak with you about having another child for a few months now, but never found the right moment. Darling, I agree with what you've said and the visit with my parents has helped me to put many of my long-held demons to rest once and for all. If I'm not pregnant now, Ian, I want to be. I love you, sweetheart."

I was speechless and we were both very emotional. We embraced a long time as the tears spilled from our eyes onto each other's shoulders.

Despite the overcast weather in June, the spirits of Medicon staff were anything but dampened. As I'd suspected would be the case, Scott Ashbury made significant changes to the organization that began to infuse hope and trust back into the hearts and minds of those who'd been neglected the most. Although losing Paul Scott from my division left me with a senior post to fill, Medicon was already beginning to experience the healing influence of an internal ombudsman, as Paul met with a few dozen employees within the first month, offering them renewed hope. For those most seriously offended, Paul had established an investigative method with checks and balances to ensure that only legitimate claims were being heard and that they were dealt with quickly and fairly. He was given the authority to recruit staff from other departments wherever and whenever necessary and, although few knew, his budget to make reparations to existing and former staff was generous. Despite the obvious concerns of encouraging litigation by going outside the company to former staff and offering compensation for their grief, suspicious dismissal, or departure, Scott Ashbury was resolute in this matter. His nature was always to act in good faith and his track record proved this. I agreed with him completely, feeling that it was time the company acknowledged its responsibility. Indeed, the history books would note that Scott was correct. Those who were wronged were given restitution and not a single lawsuit was launched.

In addition to dealing with those who'd been wronged was the challenge of repairing the culture within the company. By the end of June, as the rains gave way to sunshine and thoughts turned to summer vacations and to planning two months of child care, Medicon became an unexpected sanctuary. I believe it was Scott who actually conceived of the idea one day early in the month of June as he overheard several staff in the cafeteria express concern over what they would do with their children for the summer. After all, summer camps rarely lasted for two full months and camps were becoming prohibitively expensive for many. Most staff could only take two weeks off over the summer and, with most households having both parents working outside the home, care for the children over the summer became a thorny issue. The Medicon subsidized daycare alleviated the problem for children from 18 months to five years of age, so it was those from age six to sixteen who were the concern. Scott quickly surveyed several diners that lunch hour and grasped the magnitude of the problem. He contended that with so many staff preoccupied with their kids, it would be reasonable to expect productivity to take a nosedive over the summer. This was an opportunity for Medicon to demonstrate concern and to rally the staff together for the benefit of everyone. After instructing his assistant to send out a memo soliciting feedback regarding employees' concern over summer childcare, Scott was overwhelmed with the response.

By the third week of June, Scott announced to all office staff that as a result of the tremendous volunteer efforts of a dozen staff, a pilot summercare program would be implemented in the first week of July for a nine-week period. Albeit too late for several staff, such as myself who had made plans for their kids months in advance, the reaction was nonetheless impressive. Medicon would provide all materials for arts and crafts, and pay for field trips, transportation, and special event fees for swimming or museum visits. There would be no out-of-pocket expense for the families. However, any employee enrolling their child or children in the program, had to commit one week of their own time or their spouse's without pay to managing the children, preparing activities, and scheduling visits. The employees would staff the program and hopefully be able to spend at least part of that time with their own children, albeit in a group setting. The inevitable questions followed the announcement, but the general reaction was incredibly positive. Eighty staff signed up for the pilot year of the program, representing over one hundred and fifty children.

Groups of twenty to thirty kids were assembled by age and schedules were compiled. Scott had emphasized that the success of the initiative and its potential in future years would be contingent upon the efforts of all the volunteers and their ability as a collective to resolve conflicts. Now, a nine-week program involving one hundred and fifty children in groups of twenty to thirty with eighty parents involved, each for only a week, would have been a nightmare to organize. Also, the safety of the children would likely have been compromised. But the parents were resourceful, deputizing the older children to help with the younger and recruiting unemployed university students to assist where necessary, paying them out of a cooperative contingency fund that was established. Also, spouses of employees would often take a few days of a week of vacation time to help out. Each of these practices, coupled with the attrition in numbers of children that occurred through family vacations, enabled the program to continue uninterrupted for each of the nine weeks. The feedback couldn't have been more positive. Staff suggested they felt closer to their own families because of the time they could share doing a variety of activities they normally would not become engaged in. They added that they enjoyed working with other Medicon employees and their families and felt it drew that broader community together. And, finally, because the kids were safe and enjoying themselves, the staff were more relaxed and focused on their work than they would have been otherwise. These and other remarks were shared with Scott, myself and others at the Medicon family barbeque in mid-August, yet another new event sponsored by the company in celebration of its employees and their contributions.

Though the summercare program proved to be a wonderful initiative in itself, other improvements in morale were also made at Medicon throughout the summer months. The Soul Café, my own project, had come to life, offering a peaceful sanctuary for all staff to enjoy. Given that much of what I had envisioned for the Soul Café would in fact be responsibilities of Medicon's Human Resource department, I sought their support and involvement in the project from the onset. In fact, once construction was underway and I was confident that the vision for the project was shared by my executive colleagues, I handed ownership of it over to Human Resources. The week following the company barbeque saw the official opening of Medicon's Soul Café, a place of regeneration and growth where opportunities for staff development or meditation lay juxtaposed to delicious java. I was proud of this accomplishment, for like the family mission statement which Catherine, Kyle and I had created and framed in our home, The Soul Café was a tangible expression that legitimized the importance of every employee in Medicon's own mission statement.

With the summer drawing to a close and life at Medicon gradually responding to its new moral compass, Catherine and I decided to take a much needed and deserved break in California. Weeks earlier, we'd received a call from my sister, Marie, who thought spending a few weeks away from the pace of life in St. Louis would be a good idea. A single mother of five-year-old twins, her life was hectic to say the least, as she continued to work in the insurance business as the manager of a regional sales office, while raising her boys. Her husband had disappeared a year after the boys' birth, not to resurface for two years and only then with divorce papers. After that he'd remained in contact with Marie, visiting occasionally with the boys, never re-marrying except to his work. He made his home in New York City and Marie had arranged for the boys to visit their father there for a month from mid-August to mid-September while she stayed with us for two weeks, the first week visiting and the second watching over Kyle. This provided Catherine and me some time to be alone, an invitation we graciously accepted. The summer months had been enjoyable and we'd found many occasions for family outings, but intimacy was a rarer commodity with an active pre-adolescent bounding around the house. And though we never dwelled on the news, I was sure when Catherine realized in June that she wasn't pregnant, but simply late, she was deeply disappointed. As I reminded her at the time, though, I would revel every opportunity over the next few months to correct the situation.

Our visit with Marie was wonderful, as we hadn't seen her for over a year. But this reunion was different, for we shared a heightened awareness of each other and felt a much stronger family connection. Catherine and Marie spent considerable time together talking and laughing, sharing experiences and stories. They forged a bond over that week that spoke to their shared lifetime desire for a sister. After the week had played out, it was time for Catherine's and my much anticipated retreat to California. Two days in San Francisco, two visiting friends in Palo Alto, and a whirlwind three days driving down the coast to Monterey and Carmel then back to the Bay area. We laughed, we ate, we drank, we talked and walked until the sun went down; then we made love until it rose again. On the return leg of our vacation, we spent half a day with my brother Shawn who had landed a teaching and research post in the Botany Department at Berkeley. We met his girlfriend, toured the campus, and shared lunch at a bistro overlooking the Bay. Shawn had been so serious throughout university, he felt he could now afford to be carefree, so had no plans on settling down or getting too involved with anyone, at least not for the moment. It was great to see him. I encouraged him to keep in touch with Marie and me more often and invited him to Chicago for Christmas. Promising to consider the proposition, we said our good-byes and left for the airport.

There was something comforting about the mix of emotions we experienced once seated on the DC-10 enroute to O'Hare that Saturday afternoon. We had both just endured the pain of good-byes, but knowing that we continued to share our lives with good friends from the past evoked great happiness as did the fact we were returning to our own embracing home.

With our arrival in Chicago, came preparations for Kyle's school year, his first year at Deerborne Academy, and our good-byes to Marie, who was off to visit with Dad on the farm for a couple of weeks before returning to retrieve her boys enroute to St. Louis. September began with much excitement, and the news of Catherine's pregnancy a week later, kept the house and those within in a state of percolating bliss for weeks. Kyle was bouncing off the walls in anticipation of the arrival of a sibling. The rest of the family were equally excited for us. As for myself, I was completely absorbed in the joy of this event and overwhelmed with happiness. As for Catherine, she radiated love and health wherever she went.

By any account, my life had evolved dramatically over the preceding six months. My relationship with Catherine was closer than I could ever have imagined, our son was very happy and was soon to be joined by a new addition to our family. Our relationships with friends and family had been salvaged after years of neglect, and Catherine had repaired the fractured ties with her parents. In the face of horrific odds, I had been able to allow my personal values to be heard around the boardroom table at Medicon, and the outcome had been undeniably positive for all staff as a result. Throughout all of this turmoil, I was able to architect a strategic alliance with Biocodon, which after four short months was already promising to be the most lucrative in Medicon's history and, in the process, I had made new friends in Nathan and Helen. Perhaps most significantly, I had found the pain in my life that had plagued me for years and had taken serious steps to eliminate it. The months of therapy, counseling, reading, meditation and conversation had awakened my dormant spirit and regenerated my soul. I was a better person. Yet, there were still times when I felt overwhelmed with anxiety for no apparent reason and felt vulnerable to the material seductions of life yet again. I was afraid of repeating the mistakes of the past. While in our therapy sessions, I'd reveal these insecurities and was told they were quite natural reminders of our human frailty. Our therapist reminded us that they should be regarded as internal alarms that forewarn us of the ever-present potential of intrusions that could at any time violate our spiritual recovery. Also, on our journey through life, we must never ignore these alarms, for they serve to protect us from compromising our wholeness. Coming to better understand our insecurities gave Catherine and me renewed strength and the passion to seek new experiences for both personal and professional growth.

We channeled our energies into continued meditation, therapy, and reading while planning for our October vacation in Greece with Helen and Nathan. Nathan and I had been discussing the trip for several months, as we frequently found ourselves on the phone reviewing the progress of the new business association between the two firms. With our holiday plans confirmed, I was confident that Nathan's phone message Tuesday morning, the 14th of September, was simply to discuss the previous week's sales reports. The date was fixed in my mind thereafter because only two days earlier Catherine had celebrated her thirty-sixth birthday. Our trip to Greece was to be her birthday present. Though business was the subject of the call, it was not what I'd expected.

Having returned to my office after retrieving my morning cup of coffee, I picked up the phone and dialed Nathan's number. After our initial greetings, there was a lengthy pause in the conversation, followed by Nathan's carefully worded remarks, "I'd like to discuss a thought that I've been considering for several weeks now. But, first, are you able to talk in confidence — perhaps you would like to close your door?"

"Certainly," I responded with obvious intrigue. I rose from my desk, winked at Jackie to assure her that everything was OK, then closed my door. Returning to the phone, I assured Nathan, "OK, Nathan, my door is closed. What's on your mind?"

"Well, as you know, our alliance with Medicon has been reaping tremendous rewards for both of our companies thus far, and I am very optimistic for its future."

"Yes, I'm pleased, as well. But then success is a natural product of a relationship built on trust."

"Precisely right, my friend," Nathan continued. "And because of this success, the Biocodon Board of Directors has voted to immediately commence a process to recruit a new President and CEO for the Americas region. Biocodon will be establishing a new office in America to accelerate our growth in cancer diagnostics and therapeutics. We foresee new strategic alliances for several of our other products and perhaps developing our own sales force as well. But first we need to recruit the right person for the job."

"I see. That all sounds very exciting, but what does that have to do with me?" I inquired unassumingly.

"I believe you know, Ian. I need to find someone who knows the market, who is a seasoned business development professional, and who understands our company. But, most importantly, I need to trust this person with the future of the firm. I need to know that the person has strong moral fiber, and is not reluctant to put everything on the line in defense of their principles. That person is you. I want to offer you this position, Ian," Nathan concluded rather emphatically.

Being considered for such an important role without having sought it really bowled me over and was a big boost to my self esteem. As I sat in my office that morning searching for a reply, I realized that there was much to consider. Nathan seemed to want a response of some sort, however, so I asked, "Does this mean I'll have to be on my best behavior in Greece?"

With a laugh, he responded, "Not at all. In fact I was hoping it would be a time of great celebration."

I was on the phone for the better part of an hour discussing the particulars of the role and its responsibilities. I learned that Nathan foresaw that the person would act with considerable autonomy in creating new research partnerships and strategic alliances. In addition, the individual would oversee all current manufacturing operations in North, Central and South America, would be responsible for building the customer base in those markets, and would develop a base of operations somewhere in the United States and staff it as necessary. The position would report directly to Nathan and, in addition to being the President for the Americas region, the person would be a Senior Vice President of the firm and would have a seat on the Board. The compensation was exceptionally generous and included significant stock options. In all respects, I felt very flattered and excited at the prospect of leading a growing biotechnology company in the crucial North, Central, and South American markets. But the key ingredient in the mix was the fact that I knew and trusted Nathan, whose commitment to the firm was complete. I shared with my friend my reactions, but told him I needed to discuss the opportunity with Catherine and Kyle.

Too anxious to wait until Kyle was in bed that night, I called Catherine immediately and asked whether she could spend the afternoon with me to discuss some important but great news. It didn't take her more than a minute to make the necessary arrangements and she happily agreed to meet me at a favorite restaurant for lunch. Sharing with her my news over soup and sandwiches was exciting. We both got really enthusiastic with the prospect of an emerging new employment opportunity. In fact, Catherine explained to me that she had been thinking of leaving the consulting business to stay at home for a time after the baby was born and then opening her own business. I was absolutely supportive and realized that the new salary would easily make up for the temporary loss of her income. Another plus was that we already knew and liked Helen and Nathan. Ultimately, Catherine told me to decide with my heart, to trust in my intuition, then to work out the details. Every part of me confirmed what I wanted to do but, still, the decision to leave Medicon for a new challenge was difficult, colored by nearly a decade of committed, if bittersweet, memories. I had worked hard to build a climate of respect and hope there and had grown as a person in the process. However, the same turmoil that Catherine had felt while navigating between her past and present, was now tormenting me. Change seems inevitably to involve pain. It means challenging all that we know, all that we are comfortable with, to seek a new way. In the end, I realized that I was ready to find my new way.

Celebrating Our Souls

Despite my interest in Nathan's offer and my excitement over it, I spent several days pondering my decision. At times like this, I often found it impossible to separate my desires from what I perceived to be my responsibilities. I had felt this way throughout my life, and this point in time was no different. I considered whether I would be compromising my Medicon colleagues in some way or be demonstrating a lack of sincerity in my beliefs towards the future of the firm. I wondered whether Scott would understand or if Jackie would. As feelings of guilt tempered my enthusiasm over the promise of a wonderful new beginning, I reflected on Catherine's encouragement and also on Kyle's bravery in making the transition to a new school where he was again among the youngest, least experienced members of his community. I was constantly reminded of our family's mission statement, for it was framed and hung on the wall of the main floor hallway conspicuous to all who passed by. I must have read those words a dozen times each day, with each new reading adding resolve to my decision.

By Sunday, September 19th, I found my answer and by noon phoned Nathan at his home in Oxford to finalize the details. As expected, he was overjoyed with the news. Never before in my career had I managed to progress from first hearing of a new job to being hired for it in less than a week. But never before had Nathan Currie made me an offer, allowing my otherwise skeptical and analytical nature to be silenced. Nathan's words were wrapped in honesty and integrity and our relationship had allowed us to dispense with the usual poker-faced negotiations that often accompany compensation discussions. Nathan's offer had been more than generous. I would make nearly twice the base salary that I'd been receiving at Medicon, along with the promise of financial security through stock options. My preoccupation with Catherine's impending medical needs led me to question medical coverage, but Nathan's assurance of comprehensive benefits that rivaled those of my current employer was sufficient for me. Indeed, the focus of our dialogue was more on the business prospects and establishing the office than on my personal needs. With nothing else to consider, I asked for an employment contract to be faxed to the house the following day.

Anxiously awaiting the contract's arrival, I was very distracted on Monday. I found myself trying to keep occupied with routine business, but my mind was too charged. Passing through the lobby of Medicon's glass and chrome nerve center, I spotted Karen and Paul enjoying a cup of coffee at The Soul Café and, when invited to join them, I jumped at the chance. It seemed that they had been discussing their new roles within the firm. As ombudsman, Paul had found the previous few months rather hectic but, as most employees could attest, his approach to the issues and the outcomes achieved were both fair and expeditious. Medicon had begun to heal. As for Karen, her contributions to uncovering the chronic improprieties within Medicon were not overlooked. So, when the Finance Department had a senior post vacated and needed someone to manage the financial administration of the firm, I strongly recommended Karen. Only a month on the job as Director of Financial Administration, she had already begun implementing new internal processes and audits for sales expenses to address one of the deficiencies of the past. As I sipped my morning cup of coffee in the company of my friends, I could feel myself letting go of my tension and anxiety to the stronger forces of peace and tranquility that permeated each patron within these walls. Paul and Karen complimented me for having championed the creation of this sanctuary. I had learned that employee response cards noted an overwhelmingly positive reaction as well. However, to me nothing can beat the feeling of validation one gets directly from one's peers, so I graciously accepted Paul and Karen's acknowledgments.

Our conversation meandered like a lazy stream not needing to get anywhere in a hurry. We talked about our respective careers and how we each had taken unexpected turns at some point in time. Paul was interested in my thoughts on many of the executives, since he was now sitting amongst that group and wanted the benefit of my experience in dealing with them. We even spent a few moments revisiting the investigation and its outcome, an exercise that reminded each of us of the vulnerability of one's principles within the corporate world and the absolute need to be true to those beliefs above loyalty, pride or fear. We had each fought our personal battles, but emerged victorious, not for having defeated an adversary, but for having lived our truth without compromise.

After my leisurely visit with Paul and Karen, I headed to my office, and found that the balance of the day was tempered by the reflections of the morning which had left a lingering feeling of satisfaction within me. I found the entire day was surreal, in that part of my conscious state was engaged in my routine interactions with colleagues, whereas another part of me was observing all of this from another dimension. I was sure that this experience would be archived as a significant memory, no doubt to be replayed at another of life's junctures. And so that Monday passed, and the dichotomies of grief and happiness, immorality and soulfulness, lost opportunity and unprecedented success, isolation and community played over and over in my mind. And all the while I waited anxiously to get home to review my new employment contract.

On my way home that evening, I stopped at Deerborne Academy to pick up Kyle from baseball practice. I arrived a few minutes early and was able to watch my son strike out two of his teammates before descending from the mound. His joy of life was evident in all he did and was infectious to all those he encountered. I remember smiling from my heart at the sight of him waving excitedly as he noticed me watching from my perch on the hood of my Buick. I felt the full bounty of my life, a feeling I shared with Kyle as I embraced him after his practice and later with Catherine when she arrived home minutes after Kyle and I. After washing up, I stepped into my home office and found the fax I'd been expecting. All was in order, so I signed it and faxed it back to Nathan. Surprisingly, moments later, Nathan called to welcome me on board. I thanked him once more and informed him that Medicon would receive my letter of resignation the following day. A few minutes of friendly conversation passed as we shared our excitement over our upcoming trip to Greece. Catherine spoke briefly with Helen and then, realizing that it was past midnight in Oxford, I suggested we call them later in the week. As Catherine returned the handset to its cradle, I wrapped my arms around her and kissed her gently. We celebrated that evening as a family by going out for dinner at our favorite restaurant. After returning home and ushering our somewhat argumentative pre-teen off to bed, Catherine and I enjoyed a cup of tea and spoke animatedly into the night about our future.

Although I'd expected the news of my departure from Medicon would evoke strong emotions and make my resignation extra difficult, I was overwhelmed by the support shown me. I was able to meet with Scott at 9:00 a.m. and after explaining that I needed to embrace this challenge at this point in my career, Scott agreed that the opportunity was wonderful.

"You know, if I thought you were leaving because of the hell this company had put you through in the past, I'd disagree with your decision," Scott pointed out. "But I know you've put that behind you. Unlike many of the others around here, you stood up for your beliefs and demonstrated your passion for this firm and its future. That's a rare commodity these days."

"I only did what I knew to be right, and even that was only after prompting from Karen and Paul and a lot of soul-searching. And fortunately for Medicon, Karen and Paul remain as valued assets around here. I did what my mentor would have done, Scott, and I have no regrets. I believe this organization is as strong as it has ever been and promises continued success for its community of employees."

"You know, Ian," Scott replied, "I wish I could tell you the firm would offer you the presidency here when I leave, but that decision can become so political that I couldn't in good conscience lead you to believe something like that."

"Of course not, Scott," I said understandingly. "My departure isn't so much about Medicon or my role here, as it is about me and where I am spiritually. I've experienced considerable personal growth over this past year and when Biocodon extended this offer, a part of me deep within acknowledged that it was the right thing to do. It's as though my soul has validated this next step on my journey."

Smiling like a proud father, my friend concluded, "Well then, there it is. You must pursue this opportunity with Biocodon and, as you do, know that I wish you the greatest of success and fulfillment. I'm very proud of your achievements, Ian."

Thanking him, I began to discuss the details of my departure, including my impending vacation with Nathan and Helen that had been planned for months and the fact that I wanted Jackie to move to Biocodon with me, if she wished. Scott was very understanding and suggested that I simply take the vacation and finish up at Medicon a week later. He also thanked me for warning him about my impending offer to Jackie and, though he didn't want to lose her, he understood my loyalty and desire to maintain our working relationship. Due to the seniority of my position, the Board would need to be notified of my resignation and since I was going to be joining a firm with whom Medicon maintained a strategic alliance, a conflict of interest might be perceived. Therefore, I proposed to Scott that I resign as of that day and work only as a consultant on any matters unrelated to the Biocodon alliance for the following two weeks prior to and for one week following my vacation. Scott agreed to my recommendation and immediately dictated an internal announcement to that effect. Before leaving his office, and at Scott's insistence, I witnessed his phone conversation with the Chair of the Board of Directors when he broke the news. Although the other end of the phone line seemed less understanding, Scott clearly articulated the genuine motivation behind my departure and shared the plan for my next few weeks. With an agreement in hand, my mentor gave me until 3:00 p.m. to personally address my staff, colleagues and friends with the news, prior to his public announcement at that time. We shook hands, promised to have lunch later in the week, and I returned to my office.

With tears she found impossible to restrain, Jackie accepted the news of my resignation as bravely as she could. We had worked together successfully several years, had become good friends, and were familiar with each other's ways. She reminded me of each of these points, but knew that my mind was clear and my decision had been made. I told her what my new role would entail and how excited Catherine and I were with the possibilities, but her spirit remained deflated until I explained that I'd be grateful if she'd consider the prospect of joining me at Biocodon as my assistant. I could tell that her mind was racing, so I tore a sheet of paper off my desk pad and wrote down a figure for her to consider. It was twenty-five percent higher than her salary at Medicon, but then I knew I wouldn't have to train Jackie. Furthermore, she was highly efficient and Biocodon was presumably a higher risk employment proposition than Medicon. As I slipped the paper into her hand, I told her there would be complete medical and dental benefits and the rest would be considered as we went along. She smiled as her shaking fingers opened the folded paper and said she'd think about my offer. I asked if she could let me know by the end of the week and she nodded, wiping away her tears.

The balance of my day was spent performing the same scene over and over again as I circulated through the building informing staff and colleagues of my decision to leave. By 3:00 p.m., my mission was complete and I felt relieved that those who were closest to me over the years at Medicon had learned of my departure directly from me. Scott's voice soon came over the company's personal address system to announce my departure. He automatically commanded respect and everyone in the building broke from their routine with the sound of their president's monologue. He was generous with praise as he highlighted my accomplishments and congratulated me on being elected to my new post. He then shared the fact that I'd be operating in a consulting capacity for the five weeks that followed, providing all staff an opportunity to share their personal remarks with me. By 3:05 p.m. the announcement was over and minutes later I left the office for the last time as a permanent employee.

Although Karl and I had remained in touch over the previous few months, it had been some time since we last enjoyed each other's company. I was particularly pleased, therefore, to find my friend at the original "Soul Café" ten minutes after leaving my office. Waving to him as I entered, I proceeded straight to the counter where I ordered a cappuccino and two date squares. I offered one of the desserts to my friend who'd obviously just arrived himself, judging by the level of steamy coffee in his cup.

"Well thank you, kind sir," Karl said in response to receiving the treat. "It's wonderful to see you again, but I would've expected you to be patronizing your corporate café at this time of the day."

Having told Karl about my pride in establishing The Soul Café six weeks before, I understood his surprise in seeing me. "Well, I just needed to have some space from my colleagues for a time. You see, today I tendered my resignation and I've been speaking with people about it all day."

I spent the minutes that followed explaining to Karl my new position and my rationale for accepting Nathan's offer. In response, my friend suggested, "You know, Ian, I've made it my life's work to study animal behavior and, especially over the past year, have found humans to be most fascinating in the things they do and in their reasons for doing them. In you, for example, I've observed a tremendous evolution of spirit. You've found your truth within a world of facsimiles and fabrication and have designed a life for yourself that allows you the freedom to pursue that truth. I congratulate you on your new responsibilities and on your tenacity in being true to yourself."

"Well, thank you, Karl. That means a great deal to me," I said.

As I began to sip my beverage, Karl added, "I'm sure you've learned along your journey, Ian, that life can be reduced to a thirty second sound bite if you concede to the incessant hype of our media-driven society, or it can be filled with moments of deep, sincere reflection. I believe that meditation is critical to replenish the soul and to preserve all that is sacred in a life that can otherwise prove quite overwhelming. It is my great hope for you that your journey will be frequently visited by such contemplation."

My recollections of that afternoon remain vivid, as Karl's words impressed upon me a fundamental need of the soul that I had discovered months earlier: to embrace solitude and the opportunity for meditation. I assured my friend at the time that I wouldn't forget that which had taken me so long to learn.

When I entered the house at 5:00 p.m., I discovered Catherine had already arrived and started dinner. Wanting to know how my day had progressed, I sat down on a kitchen chair and explained in detail the day's events as she prepared a salad. After dinner, I began to phone my family and friends to share the news with them. Some of our friends were still unaware of the impending addition to the family, so after I'd finished telling my news, Catherine took the phone and reported our family news. She was about eight weeks pregnant, though still not showing. At 9:30 p.m., I slipped away from the living room, where Catherine was busy on the phone, to say good night to Kyle. I found him in bed engrossed in a book when I entered his room.

"Hey, sport, it's time to sleep," I said. "What are you reading?"

"It's Huckleberry Finn. You know, in a way he reminds me of you, Dad, traveling to different places, meeting new people... Hey, are you still gonna travel in your new job? I miss you when you're gone, but I also really like hearing your stories when you come back, and I like the stuff you bring me, too."

"Oh yeah, I'm sure I'll be traveling, perhaps more than any of us want, at least for the first while," I answered. Looking around Kyle's room, I could sense the pride he had in displaying the presents I had bought for him over the years.

"Hopefully not too much, though, ok? You know I'm proud of you, don't you, Dad?" Kyle uttered matter-of-factly.

"Well, that's a nice thing to say, Kyle. Why are you proud of me?" I asked.

"'Cuz I know that this is a big promotion for you and you work hard, so you deserve it. That's why," was his straightforward answer.

"Thanks, son. That means a lot to me. Now, it's time for bed. I love you Kyle. Sleep well," I told him with a hug.

"I love you too, Dad. G'night."

As I returned to my wife's side, I remember thinking: out of the mouths of babes come the most comforting, touching words, words carried on the backs of our spirits, words that fill our souls.

The weeks that followed left me with an odd feeling of disassociation at work. There were meetings to attend and discussions of succession plans. Those employees reporting to me directly required performance appraisals and I needed to ensure that appropriate leadership was provided for all departments and for each project. As planned, Scott and I met for lunch a few days after the announcement. He added a few additional details to my agenda and also asked me whether I knew of any potential internal successor to my position. I felt that Medicon would be better served by recruiting someone from outside the firm despite its corporate policy to promote from within. Scott appreciated my candor and spent the rest of our lunch advising me on investment decisions relative to my Medicon stock and my company pension. When I returned from lunch, I invited Jackie to have a seat in my office as she had asked to speak with me. She had prepared a list of questions pertaining to my offer and I answered them as completely as possible. Her inquiries revealed the fact that she had been considering my proposition very seriously. I was flattered by her thoughtful suggestions and by the time she'd invested in this process. After the last question was answered, she took a deep breath and asked when she could start. Delighted by her decision, I told her I'd draft up a letter of employment that evening and, if she found it agreeable, she could start two weeks later, on Monday, October 12th. Realizing I'd be away in Greece at that time, I knew I could count on Jackie's talents in assessing a number of office properties in the area and handling a few other administrative issues from her home. With her agreement, we exchanged smiles, shook hands, then hugged.

I made a formal offer of employment to Jackie the following day and, with this, she tendered her resignation at Medicon. A similar wave of excitement and emotion was initiated as a result and, at Scott's insistence, a joint departure party was planned for the following week to honor Jackie's and my own contributions to the firm over the years. It was held in the cafeteria on the Friday afternoon prior to my vacation and was open to all Medicon staff. A barbeque was provided along with party favors and dessert and, as the afternoon progressed, the sound of champagne corks could be heard. We were both presented with beautiful momentos to recognize our time at Medicon and almost all eyes in the room watered-up as Jackie expressed her thanks and good fortune for having encountered so many wonderful people in her life during her years at Medicon. It was a fitting celebration of accomplishment and friendship.

Within two days of the party, Catherine and I were loading a taxi to take to the airport enroute to Athens. Kyle would be staying with our good friends and neighbors two houses away where he would have an opportunity to be with one of his closest school friends day and night. As he watched us pack the car, his expression seemed to be one of excitement at the prospect of being on his own adventure, tempered by obligation to feel saddened by the two-week absence of his parents. But we were certain the latter would soon be displaced by an afternoon with his friends, so with a big hug and a kiss from our son, we jumped into the car and raced to the airport, confident he was in good hands.

After stopping in New York to refuel and pick up passengers, our flight was non-stop to Greece. We managed to sleep several hours on the plane, so were in reasonable form when we found Nathan and Helen at the arrival's gate at 7:00 a.m. Monday morning. Our reunion was an affirmation of our souls. We laughed, we cried, we congratulated each other. When our hunger caught up to our humor, we found a restaurant and ate, toasting to our health and friendship. We toured the ancient city for a few days, buying little momentos for each other from the animated street vendors we frequently encountered, then boarded a cruise ship destined for the Greek islands. Mykonos, Santorini, Crete— we bathed in the sun in each. Catherine and I found time for ourselves as we explored the streets of villages that time had forgotten.

Each day the sea and the sky shared the same palette allowing the horizon to escape notice except to those who held their loved ones patiently as the brilliant sun exploded with pinks and oranges and yellows and blues upon setting down into the sea. Catherine and I were so joyous at these moments for they seemed to be a fitting acknowledgment of another perfect day, another day of fulfilled dreams and inner peace. But perhaps most endearing to us during those days on the Aegean Sea wasn't the splendor of the setting, but rather the recognition that we didn't need to escape to another world or to be inspired by some unique vista to find peace in our souls or to feel whole. These gifts were now a part of our everyday lives. They could be found in our routine practices if we allowed ourselves to grow and to evolve. Soulful regeneration was ours through our community of friends and family, through moments of solitude and meditation, through personal achievements, and through a spiritual existence that permitted our values to shepherd us through life.

Our time with Nathan and Helen was all too short, but we found solace in the promise of more frequent visits as a result of the new American Biocodon operations. Upon our return home, I found myself busy finalizing my commitments to Medicon, while beginning to organize for the commencement of Biocodon operations in America. Jackie had eased my workload considerably by having scouted out several acceptable office locations where space could be leased and future growth accommodated. I asked Catherine to accompany me on several of the site visits to enjoy the benefit of her intuition and experience in these matters gained over her years as a consultant. I was able to secure space and arrange for all necessary lease-hold improvements to be completed within one month. Meanwhile, Jackie handled the other logistics to enable us to occupy the new American home of Biocodon within days of the completion of our space.

Once I had finished my duties with Medicon, I was able to dedicate my full attention to my new responsibilities. After a few trips to Oxford to meet with Nathan, the Board, and several investigators, I became focused in pursuit of three critical business opportunities, including the design of two licensing agreements for Biocodon products and the establishment of a research partnership with the Dana Farber Cancer Centre in Boston.

But work was not my sole passion in life. Catherine and I continued to exercise together, both in body and spirit. We attended therapy sessions once a month and therein strengthened our resolve to preserve happiness in our lives. Catherine found an outlet for her passion through painting and, moved by the life that grew within her, began to create what was to become a beautiful collection of impressionistic pieces. Each painting symbolized a moment of soulful celebration. Kyle, on the other hand, was absorbed in hockey and school life, including rehearsals for his stage debut in a school production of Death of a Salesman. Kyle's part was modest, portraying a young Biff, but he was excited nonetheless. Reminded of the plot as I helped my son with his lines, I reflected on the tragedy inherent in failing to recognize what is truly important in life. I hoped that my new approach to living would serve as a positive example for my son. All told, our lives were full and sometimes hectic, but we had learned to balance our time and to be good to ourselves.

By Thanksgiving Day, we were blessed by the company of Shawn, Marie and her boys, my father, Catherine's parents, and the entire Currie household. We had much to be grateful for, and we each took turns around the dinner table expressing our thanks. The following Monday, November 29, my family, friends, and a few stalwart financial reporters interested in both a good biotechnology story and a free buffet, descended upon the new American offices of Biocodon. With great delight and pride, Nathan and I shared in the ribbon-cutting exercise. Largely a result of Jackie's diligent efforts, we'd managed to meet the aggressive timelines I'd established for our grand opening. Amidst the revelry of that day, where my family and closest friends gathered in music and song and laughter, filling the air with triumphant joy, I felt a most fulfilling peace.

Two weeks have passed since that delightful gathering. The first snow of the season has kissed the Earth and we've begun preparations for Christmas. It was last night, during a visit with our therapist, that Catherine and I were asked to consider sharing our experiences with another couple who'd reached a crisis in their lives. Anxious to help others find what we'd found, I've spent the last several hours pouring over the previous nine months of my life.

I think about the benchmarks I've passed during this journey. I'm an ordinary guy, with an ordinary family. I took my son to hockey practice and baseball tryouts. My wife and I both worked outside the home because we wanted more for our family than our parents had provided. We had few financial problems, seldom fought, and had a great child.

But, then, we seldom really talked and rarely really listened to each other. We had one child because our schedules wouldn't permit us more. And the money was never enough to conceal the nakedness of our spirits. We shamefully hid the fact that we didn't know how to provide spiritually for our family the way our parents had. The fact was that somewhere along the line we'd surrendered ourselves to the heady seductions of life and, in the process, had lost our way. Like a child who lets go of his mother's hand for an instant and suddenly finds himself in a cyclone of strangers rushing all around him, I too had been stricken and overwhelmed by fear. My inner compass was muted. I felt betrayed by life. Sickened, exhausted, hollow, my melancholy had dimmed the brightest moments. I had abandoned my soul as innocently as the child had his mother's hand. But, when I finally allowed myself to recognize my negligence, when I eventually learned to acknowledge and feel my pain, only then did I begin what was to become my process of healing.

I pause to consider whether the healing is complete. I suspect there will be continual nurturing, growth, and rebirth as long as I remain true to this process. In fact, I believe it's the ability to embrace the process of spiritual evolution from where we've been to where we're going that enables us continually to achieve wholeness in an ever-changing world. To liberate our spirits, to channel our soulful energies, and to replenish ourselves amidst this crazy, hectic, materialistic world in which we live, these are the lessons I believe we must come to learn. Our challenge lies in permitting ourselves the freedom to learn them. We need sanctuaries to nurture ourselves and our souls and to celebrate the human spirit. This is what The Soul Café has been for me. It's been a place to be at peace, to evolve, and to dream of my potential. It was there that I first found real love, that is, love for myself. It was there that I found my pain. It was there that I released the potential within me to change. Even now, I relish the time I spend there. More importantly, however, I am relishing the time between visits. This place has helped me to rediscover my spirit, and to catch a glimpse of freedom. But beyond that, The Soul Café has inspired me with reverence for the joy of the journey.

Epilogue

In having read this book, it is my hope it may serve as a catalyst for you to pose some questions about your own life. Perhaps take a moment to ask yourself the following:

Who am I?

What is my pain?

What is most important to me in my life? Why?

Where am I in my life in relation to where I wish to be?

How can I achieve balance and a sense of wholeness?

How can I make a difference?

As you ponder these questions, never doubt that the answers exist for you. Whether in the silence of the soul, the fellowship of friends and family, or the comfort of a coffee shop, seek them out, and in Gandi's words, "Be the change you want to see in the world."

If you wish to share your own related stories, or to pose questions or comments, please visit our website at www.soulzatwork.com

Many thanks,

David McLean

Additional Information

For further information about the author, to arrange speaking engagements, to order additional copies of this book, to share your own stories, or to comment on *The Soul Café* please visit our web site at:

www.soulzatwork.com

The cover for this book was designed by Domenic Sallese of SALT Advertising and Design. For his assistance in meeting your creative design challenges, please email Domenic at the following address:

salt@look.ca

The back cover photograph was created by Kevin Spreek-meester of Blue Door Photography/Communications. For world-class photography and innovative marketing communications solutions, please visit Kevin at the following address:

www.bluedoorphoto.com